The Prince

By

Niccolò Machiavelli

The Prince

By

Niccolò Machiavelli

This book was written in the prevailing style of that period. Language and spelling have been left original in an effort to give the full flavor of this classic work.

Bottom of the Hill Publishing

Memphis, TN

www.BottomoftheHillPublishing.com

ISBN: 978-1-61203-109-5

The Prince

To the Magnificent Laurence son to Peter of Medicis Health

They that desire to ingratiate themselves with a Prince, commonly use to offer themselves to his view, with things of that nature as such persons take most pleasure and delight in: whereupon we see they are many times presented with Horses and Armies, cloth of gold, precious stones, and such like ornaments, worthy of their greatness. Having then a mind to offer up my self to your Magnificence, with some testimony of my service to you, I found nothing in my whole inventory, that I think better of, or more esteem, than the knowledge of great mens actions, which I have learned by a long experience of modern affairs, and a continual reading of those of the ancients. Which, now that I have with great diligence long worked it out, and thoroughly sifted, I commend to your Magnificence. And, however I may well think this work unworthy of your view; yet such is your humanity, that I doubt not but it shall find acceptance, considering, that for my part I am not able to tender a greater gift, than to present you with the means, whereby in a very short time you may be able to understand all that, which I, in the space of many years, and with many sufferances and dangers, have made proof and gained the knowledge of. And this work I have not set forth either with elegancy of discourse or stile, nor with any other ornament whereby to captivate the reader, as others use, because I would not have it gain its esteem from elsewhere than from the truth of the matter, and the gravity of the subject. Nor can this be thought presumption, if a man of humble and low condition venture to dilate and discourse upon the governments of Princes; for even as they that with their pensils designe out countries, get themselves into the plains below to consider the nature of the mountains, and other high places above; and again to consider the plains below, they get up to the tops of the mountains; in like manner to understand the nature of the people, it is fit to be a Prince; and to know well the dispositions of Princes, sutes best with the understanding of a subject. Your Magnificence then may be pleased, to receive this small present, with the same mind that I send it; which if you shall throughly peruse and consider, you shall perceive therein that I exceedingly wish, that you may attain to that greatness, which your own fortune, and your excellent endowments promise you: and if your Magnificence from the very point of your Highness shall sometime cast your eyes upon these inferior places, you shall see how undeservedly I undergo an extreme and continual despight of Fortune.

How Many Sorts of Principalities There Are, and How Many Ways They Are Attained

All States, all Dominions that have had, or now have rule over men, have been and are, either Republiques or Principalities. Principalities are either hereditary, whereof they of the blood of the Lord thereof have long time been Princes; or else they are new; and those that are new, are either all new, as was the Dutchy of Millan to Francis Sforce; or are as members adjoined to the hereditary State of the Prince that gains it; as the Kingdom of Naples is to the King of Spain. These Dominions so gotten, are accustomed either to live under a Prince, or to enjoy their liberty; and are made conquest of, either with others forces, or ones own, either by fortune, or by valor.

Of Hereditary Principalities

I will not here discourse of Republiques, because I have other where treated of them at large: I will apply my self only to a Principality, and proceed, while I weave this web, by arguing thereupon, how these Principallities can be governed and maintained. I say then that in States of inheritance, and accustomed to the blood of their Princes, there are far fewer difficulties to keep them, than in the new: for it suffices only not to transgress the course his Ancestors took, and so afterward to temporize with those accidents that can happen; that if such a Prince be but of ordinary industry, he shall always be able to maintain himself in his State, unless by some extraordinary or excessive power he be deprived thereof; and when he had lost it, upon the least sinister chance that befalls the usurper, he recovers it again. We have in Italy the Duke of Ferrara for example hereof, who was of ability to resist the Venetians, in the year 84, and to withstand Pope Julius in the tenth for no other reason, than because he had of old continued in that rule; for the natural Prince hath fewer occasions, and less hed to give offence, whereupon of necessity he must be more beloved; and unless it be that some extravagant vices of his bring him into hatred, it is agreeable to reason, that naturally he should be well beloved by his own subjects: and in the antiquity and continuation of the Dominion, the remembrances and occasions of innovations are quite extinguished: for evermore one change leaves a kind of breach or dent, to fasten the building of another.

Of Mixed Principalities

But the difficulties consist in the new Principality; and first, if it be not all new, but as a member, so that it may be termed altogether as mixed; and the variations thereof proceed in the first place from a natural difficulty, which we commonly finde in all new Principalities; for men do willingly change their Lord, believing to better their condition; and this belief causes them to take armies against him that rules over them, whereby they deceive themselves, because they find after by experience, they have made it worse: which depends upon another natural and ordinary necessity, forcing him always to offend those, whose Prince he newly becomes, as well by his soldiers he is put to entertain upon them as by many other injuries, which a new conquest draws along with it; in such manner as thou findest all those thine enemies, whom thou hast endangered in the seizing of that Principality, and afterwards canst not keep them thy friends that have seated the in it, for not being able to satisfy them according to their expectations, nor put in practice strong remedies against them, being obliged to them. For however one be very well provided with strong armies, yet hath he always need of the favor of the inhabitants in the Country, to enter thereinto. For these reasons, Lewis the twelfth, King of France, suddenly took Milan, and as soon lost it; and the first time Lodwick his own forces served well enough to wrest it out of his hands; for those people that had opened him the gates, finding themselves deceived of their opinion, and of that future good which they had promised themselves, could not endure the distastes the new Prince gave them. True it is, that Countries that have rebelled again the second time, being recovered, are harder lost; for their Lord, taking occasion from their rebellion, is less respective of persons, but cares only to secure himself, by punishing the delinquents, to clear all suspicions, and to provide for himself where he thinks he is weakest: so that if to make France lose Milan the first time, it was enough for Duke Lodwick to make some small stir only upon the confines; yet afterwards, before they could make him lose it the second time, they had need of the whole world together against him, and that all his armies should be wasted and driven out of Italy; which proceeded from the forenamed causes: however though both the first and second time it was taken from him. The general causes of the first we have treated of; it remains now that we see those of the second; and set down the remedies that he had, or any one else can have that should chance to be in those terms he was, whereby he might be able to maintain himself better in his conquest than the King of France did. I say therefore, that these States which by Conquest are annexed to the ancient states of their conqueror, are either of the same province and the same language, or otherwise; and when they are, it is very easy to hold them, especially when they are not used to live free; and to enjoy them securely, it is enough to have extinguished the Princes line who ruled over them: For in other matters, allowing them their ancient conditions, and there being not much difference of manners betwixt them, men ordinarily live quiet enough; as we have seen that Burgundy did, Britany, Gascony, and Normandy, which so long

time continued with France: for however there be some difference of language between them, yet can they easily com-
port one with another; and whosoever makes the conquest of
them, meaning to hold them, must have two regards; the
first, that the race of their former Prince be quite extinguished; the other, that he change nothing, neither in their
laws nor taxes, so that in a very short time they become one
entire body with their ancient Principality. But when any
States are gained in a Province disagreeing in language, manners, and orders, here are the difficulties, and here is there
need of good fortune, and great industry to maintain them;
and it would be one of the best and liveliest remedies, for the
Conqueror to goe in person and dwell there; this would make
the possession hereof more secure and durable; as the Turk
hath done in Greece, who among all the other courses taken
by him for to hold that State, had he not gone thither himself
in person to dwell, it had never been possible for him to have
kept it: for abiding there, he sees the disorders growing in
their beginnings, and forthwith can remedy them; whereas
being not there present, they are heard of when they are
grown to some height, and then is there no help for them.
Moreover, the Province is not pillaged by the officers thou
sendest thither: the subjects are much satisfied of having
recourse to the Prince near at hand, whereupon have they
more reason to love him, if they mean to be good; and intending to do otherwise, to fear him: and foreign Princes will be
well aware how they invade that State; insomuch, that making his abode there, he can very hardly lose it. Another remedy, which is also a better, is to send Colonies into one or two
places, which may be as it were the keys of that State; for it
is necessary either to do this, or to maintain there many
horse and foot. In these colonies the Prince makes no great
expense, and either without his charge, or at a very small
rate, he may both send and maintain them; and gives offence
only to them from whom he takes their fields and houses, to
bestow them on those new inhabitants who are but a very
small part of that State; and those that he offends, remaining
dispersed and poor, can never hurt him: and all the rest on

one part, have no offence given them, and therefore a small matter keeps them in quiet: on the other side, they are wary not to err, for fear it befalls not them, as it did those that were dispoild. I conclude then, that those colonies that are not chargeable, are the more trusty, give the less offence; and they that are offended, being but poor and scattered, can do but little harm, as I have said; for it is to be noted, that men must either be dallied and flattered with all, or else be quite crushed; for they revenge themselves of small damages; but of great ones they are not able; so that when wrong is done to any man, it ought so to be done, that it need fear no return of revenge again. But in lieu of Colonies, by maintaining soldiers there, the expense is great; for the whole revenues of that State are to be spent in the keeping of it; so the conquest proves but a loss to him that hath got it, and endamages him rather; for it hurts that whole State to remove the army from place to place, of which annoyance every one hath a feeling, and so becomes enemy to the; as they are enemies, I wis, who are outraged by the in their own houses, whensoever they are able to do the mischief. Every way then is this guard unprofitable. Besides, he that is in a different Province, (as it is said) should make himself Head and defender of his less powerful neighbors, and devise always to weaken those that are more mighty therein, and take care that upon no chance there enter not any foreigner as mighty as himself; for it will always come to pass, that they shall be brought in by those that are discontented, either upon ambition, or fear; as the Etolians brought the Romans into Greece; and they were brought into every country they came, by the Natives; and the course of the matter is, that so soon as a powerful Stranger enters a country, all those that are the less powerful there, cleave to him, provoked by an envy they beare him that is more mighty than they; so that for these of the weaker sort, he may easily gain them without any pains: for presently all of them together very willingly make one lump with that he hath gotten: He hath only to beware that these increase not their strengths, nor their authorities, and so he shall easily be able by his own forces, and their assistance, to take down those that are mighty, and remain himself absolute arbiter of that Country. And he that plays not well this part, shall quickly lose what he hath gotten; and while he holds it, shall find therein a great many troubles and vexations. The Romans in the Provinces they seiz'd on, observed well these points, sent colonies thither, entertained the weaker sort, without augmenting any thing their power, abated the forces of those that were mighty, and permitted not any powerful foreigner to gain too much reputation there. And I will content my self only with the country of Greece for example hereof. The Achayans and Etolians were entertained by them, the Macedons Kingdom was brought low, Antiochus was driven thence, nor ever did the Achayans or Etolians deserts prevail so far for them, that they would ever promise to enlarge their State, nor the persuasions of Philip induce them ever to be his friends, without bringing him lower; nor yet could Antiochus his power make them ever consent that he should hold any State in that country: for the Romans did in these cases that which all judicious Princes ought to do, who are not only to have regard unto all present mischiefs, but also to the future, and to provide for those with all industry; for by taking order for those when they are afar off, it is easy to prevent them; but by delaying till they come near hand to the, the remedy comes too late; for this malignity is grown incurable: and it befalls this, as the physicians say of the hectic fever, that in the beginning it is easily cur'd, but hardly known; but in the course of time, not having been known in the beginning, nor cured, it becomes easy to know, but hard to cure. Even so falls it out in matters of State; for by knowing it aloof off (which is given only to a wise man to do) the mischiefs that then spring up, are quickly helped; but when, for not having been perceived, they are suffered to increase, so that every one sees them, there is then no cure for them: therefore the Romans, seeing these inconvenients afar off, always prevented them, and never suffered them to follow; for to escape a war, because they knew that a war is not undertaken, but deferred for anothers advantage; therefore would they rather make a war with

Philip and Antiochus in Greece, to the end it should not afterwards be made with them in Italy, though for that time they were able to avoid both the one and the other, which they thought not good to do: nor did they approve of that saying that is ordinarily in the mouths of the Sages of our days, to enjoy the benefits of the present time; but that rather, to take the benefit of their valor and wisdom; for time drives forward everything, and may bring with it as well good as evil, and evil as good. But let us return to France, and examine if any of the things prescribed have been done by them: and we will speak of Lewis, and not of Charles, as of whom by reason of the long possession he held in Italy we better knew the ways he went: and you shall see he did the clean contrary to what should have been done by him that would maintain a State of different Language and conditions. King Lewis was brought into Italy by the Venetians ambition, who would have gotten for their shares half the State of Lombardy: I will not blame his coming, or the course he took, because he had a mind to begin to set a foot in Italy; but having not any friends in the country, all gates being barred against him, by reason of King Charles his carriage there, he was constrained to join friendship with those he could; and this consideration well taken, would have proved lucky to him, when in the rest of his courses he had not committed any error. The King then having conquered Lombardy, recovered presently all that reputation that Charles had lost him; Genua yielded to him, the Florentines became friends with him; the Marquess of Mantua, the Duke of Ferrara, the Bentivolti, the Lady of Furli, the Lord of Faenza, Pesaro Rimino, Camerino, and Piombino, the Lucheses, Pisans and Sienses, every one came and offered him friendship: then might the Venetians consider the rashness of the course they had taken, who, only to get into their hands two Towns in Lombardy, made the King Lord of two thirds in Italy. Let any man now consider with how small difficulty could the King have maintained his reputation in Italy, if he had followed these afore named rules, and secured and defended those his friends, who because their number was great, and they weak and fearful, some of the Church, and others of the Venetians were always forced to hold with him, and by their means he might easily have been able to secure himself against those that were mightiest: but he was no sooner got into Milan, than he took a quite wrong course, by giving aid to Pope Alexander, to seize upon Romania, and perceiv'd not that by this resolution he weakened himself, ruining his own friends, and those had cast themselves into his bosom, making the Church puissant, by adding to their Spiritual power, they gained their authority, and so much temporal estate. And having once got out of the way, he was constrained to go on forward; insomuch as to stop Alexanders ambition, and that he should not become Lord of all Tuscany, of force he was to come into Italy: and this sufficed him not, to have made the Church mighty, and taken away his own friends; but for the desire he had to get the Kingdom of Naples, he divided it with the King of Spain: and where before he was the sole arbitre of Italy, he brought in a competitor, to the end that all the ambitious persons of that country, and all that were ill affected to him, might have otherwhere to make their recourse: and whereas he might have left in that Kingdom some Vice-King of his own, he took him from thence, to place another there, that might afterward chace him thence. It is a thing indeed very natural and ordinary, to desire to be of the getting hand: and always when men undertake it, if they can effect it, they shall be prais'd for it, or at least not blam'd: but when they are not able, and yet will undertake it, here lies the blame, here is the error committed. If France then was able with her own power to assail the Kingdom of Naples, she might well have done it; but not being able, she should not have divided it: and if the division she made of Lombardy with the Venetians, deserv'd some excuse, thereby to set one foot in Italy; yet this merits blame, for not being excused by that necessity. Lewis then committed these five faults; extinguished the feebler ones, augmented the State of another that was already powerful in Italy, brought thereinto a very puissant foreigner, came not thither himself to dwell there, nor planted any colonies there: which faults while he liv'd, he could not but be the worse for; yet all could not have gone so ill, had he not committed the sixth, to take from the Venetians their State; for if he had not enlarg'd the Churches territories nor brought the Spaniard into Italy, it had bin necessary to take them lower; but having first taken those other courses, he should never have given way to their destruction; for while they had been strong, they would always have kept the others off from venturing on the conquest of Lombardy. For the Venetians would never have given their consents thereto, unless they should have been made Lords of it themselves; and the others would never have taken it from France, to give it them: and then they would never have dar'd to go and set upon them both together. And if any one should say, that King Lewis yielded Romania to Alexander, and the Kingdom of Naples to Spain, to avoid a war; I answer with the reasons above alleged, that one should never suffer any disorder to follow, for avoiding of a war; for that war is not sav'd, but put off to thy disadvantage. And if any others argue, that the King had given his word to the Pope, to do that exploit for him, for dissolving of his marriage, and for giving the Cardinals Cap to him of Roan; I answer with that which hereafter I shall say touching Princes words, how they ought to be kept. King Lewis then lost Lombardy, for not having observ'd some of those terms which others used, who have possessed themselves of countries, and desir'd to keep them. Nor is this any strange thing, but very ordinary and reasonable: and to this purpose I spake at Nantes with that French Cardinal, when Valentine (for so ordinarily was Cæsar Borgia Pope Alexanders son call'd) made himself master of Romania; for when the Cardinal said to me, that the Italians understood not the feats of war; I answered, the Frenchmen understood not matters of State: for had they been well vers'd therein, they would never have suffer'd the Church to have grown to that greatness. And by experience we have seen it, that the power hereof in Italy, and that of Spain also, was caused by France, and their own ruin proceeded from themselves. From whence a general rule may be taken, which never, or very seldom fails, That he that gives the means to another to become powerful, ruins himself; for that power is caused by him either with his industry, or with his force; and as well the one as the other of these two is suspected by him that is grown puissant.

Wherefore Darius His Kingdom Taken by Alexander, Rebelled Not Against Alexanders Successors after His Death

The difficulties being consider'd, which a man hath in the maintaining of a State new gotten, some might marvel how it came to pass, that Alexander the great subdued all Asia in a few years; and having hardly possessed himself of it, died; whereupon it seemed probable that all that State should have rebelled; nevertheless his Successors kept the possession of it, nor found they other difficulty in holding it, than what arose among themselves through their own ambition. I answer, that all the Principalities whereof we have memory left us, have been governed in two several manners; either by a Prince, and all the rest Vassals, who as ministers by his favor and allowance, do help to govern that Kingdom; or by a Prince and by Barons, who not by their Princes favor, but by the antiquity of blood hold that degree. And these kinds of Barons have both states of their own, and Vassals who acknowledge them for their Lords; and bare them a true natural affection. Those States that are govern'd by a Prince and by Vassals, have their Prince ruling over them with more authority; for in all his country, there is none acknowledged for superior, but himself: and if they yield obedience to any one else, it is but as to his minister and officer, nor beare they him any particular good will. The examples of these two different Governments now in our days, are, the Turk, and the King of France. The Turks whole Monarchy is govern'd by one Lord, and the rest are all his Vassals; and dividing his whole Kingdom into divers Sangiacques or Governments, he sends several thither, and those he chops and changes, as he pleases. But the King of France is seated in the midst of a multitude of Lords, who of old have been acknowledg'd for such by their subjects, and being belov'd by them, enjoy their preheminencies; nor can the King take their States from them without danger. He then that considers the one and the other of these two States, shall find difficulty in the conquest of the Turks State; but when once it is subdu'd, great facility to hold it. The reasons of these difficulties in taking of the Turks Kingdom from him, are, because the Invader cannot be called in by the Princes of that Kingdom, nor hope by the rebellion of those which he hath about him, to be able to facilitate his enterprise: which proceeds from the reasons aforesaid; for they being all his slaves, and oblig'd to him, can more hardly be corrupted; and put case they were corrupted, little profit could he get by it, they not being able to draw after them any people, for the reasons we have shewed: whereupon he that assails the Turk, must think to find him united; and must rather rely upon his own forces, than in the others disorders: but when once he is overcome and broken in the field, so that he cannot repair his armies, there is nothing else to be doubted than the Royal blood, which being once quite out, there is none else left to be feared, none of the others having any credit with the people. And as the conqueror before the victory could not hope in them; so after it, ought he not to fear them. The contrary falls out in Kingdoms governed as is that of France: for it is easy to be entered by the gaining of any Baron in the Kingdom; for there are always some malcontents to be found, and those that are glad of innovation. Those for the reasons alledg'd are able to open the a way into that State, and to further thy victory, which afterwards to make good to the, draws with it exceeding many difficulties, as well with those that have aided the, as those thou hast supprest. Nor is it enough for the to root out the Princes race: for there remaine still those Lords who quickly will be the ring-leaders of new changes; and in case thou art not able to content these, nor extinguish them, thou losest that State, whensoever the occasion is offered. Now if thou shalt consider what sort of government that of Darius was, thou shalt find it like to the Turks dominion, and therefore Alexander was necessitated first to defeat him utterly, and drive him out of the field; after which victory Darius being dead, that State was left secure to Alexander, for the reasons we treated of before: and his successors, had they continued in amity, might have enjoy'd it at ease: nor ever arose there in that Kingdom other tumults, than those they themselves stir'd up. But of the States that are order'd and grounded as that of France, it is impossible to become master at such ease: and from hence grew the frequent rebellions of Spain, France, and Greece against the Romans, by reason of the many Principalities those States had: whereof while the memory lasted, the Romans were always doubtful of the possession of them; but the memory of them being quite wip't out, by the power and continuance of the Empire, at length they enjoy'd it securely; and they also were able afterwards fighting one with another, each of one them to draw after them the greater part of those provinces, according as their authority had gain'd them credit therein: and that because the blood of their ancient Lords was quite spent, they acknowledg'd no other but the Romans. By the consideration then of these things, no man will marvaile that Alexander had so little trouble to keep together the State of Asia; and that others have had such great difficulties to maintain their conquest, as Pyrrhus, and many others; which proceeds not from the small or great valor of the conquerour, but from the difference of the subject.

In What Manner Cities and Principalities Are to Be Govern'd, Which, Before They Were Conquer'd, Liv'd under Their Own Laws

When those States that are conquered, as it is said, have been accustomed to live under their own Laws, and in liberty, there are three ways for a man to hold them. The first is to demolish all their strong places; the other, personally to goe and dwell there; the third, to suffer them to live under their own Laws, drawing from them some tribute, and creating therein an Oligarchy, that may continue it in thy service: for that State being created by that Prince, knows it cannot consist without his aid and force, who is like to doe all he can to maintain it; and with more facility is a City kept by means of her own Citizens, which hath been used before to live free, than by any other way of keeping. We have for example the Spartans and the Romans; the Spartans held Athens and Thebes, creating there an Oligarchy: yet they lost it. The Romans to be sure of Capua, Carthage, and Numantia, dismantell'd them quite, and so lost them not: they would have kept Greece as the Spartans had held them, leaving them free, and letting them enjoy their own Laws; and it prospered not with them: so that they were forc'd to deface many Cities of that province to hold it. For in truth there is not a surer way to keep them under, than by demolishments; and whoever becomes master of a City used to live free, and dismantells it not, let him look himself to be ruin'd by it; for it always in time of rebellion takes the name of liberty for refuge, and the ancient orders it had; which neither by length of time, nor for any favours afforded them, are ever forgotten; and for any thing that can be done, or order'd, unless the inhabitants be disunited and dispers'd, that name is never forgotten, nor those customs: but presently in every chance recourse is thither made: as Pisa did after so many years that she had been subdu'd by the Florentines. But when the Cities or the Provinces are accustomed to live under a Prince, and that whole race is quite extirpated: on one part being used to obey; on the other, not having their old Prince; they agree not to make one from among themselves: they know not how to live in liberty, in such manner that they are much slower to take armies; and with more facility may a Prince gain them, and secure himself of them. But in Republiques there is more life in them, more violent hatred, more earnest desire of revenge; nor does the remembrance of the ancient liberty ever leave them, or suffer them to rest; so that the safest way, is, either to ruin them, or dwell among them.

Of New Principalities, That Are Conquer'd by Ones Own Armies and Valor

Let no man marvaile, if in the discourse I shall make of new Principalities, both touching a Prince, and touching a State, I shall allege very famous examples: for seeing men almost always walk in the pathes beaten by others, and proceed in their actions by imitation; and being that others ways cannot be exactly follow'd, nor their virtues, whose pattern thou set'st before the, attain'd unto; a wise man ought always to tread the footsteps of the worthyst persons, and imitate those that have been the most excellent: to the end that if his virtue arrive not thereto, at least it may yield some favour thereof, and doe as good Archers use, who thinking the place they intend to hit, too far distant, and knowing how farr the strength of their bow will carry, they lay their aim a great deal higher than the mark; not for to hit so high with their arrow, but to be able with the help of so high an aime to reach the place they shoot at. I say, that in Principalities wholly new, where there is a new Prince, there is more and lesse difficulty in maintaining them, as the virtue of their Conquerour is greater or lesser. And because this success, to become a Prince of a private man, presupposes either virtue, or fortune; mee thinks the one and other of these two things in part should mitigate many difficulties; however he that hath lesse stood upon fortune, hath maintain'd himself the better. Moreover it somewhat facilitates the matter in that the Prince is constrain'd, because he hath not other dominions, in person to come and dwell there. But to come to these who by their own virtues, and not by fortune, attain'd to be Princes; the excellentest of these are Moses, Cyrus, Romulus, Theseus, and such like; and though of Moses we are not to reason, he only executing the things that were commanded him by God; yet merits he well to be admir'd, were it only for that grace that made him worthy to converse with God. But considering Cyrus, and the others, who either got or founded Kingdoms, we shall find them all admirable; and if there particular actions and Lawes be throughly weigh'd, they will not appear much differing from those of Moyses, which he receiv'd from so Sovraigne an instructer. And examining their lives and actions, it will not appear, that they had other help of fortune, than the occasion, which presented them with the matter wherein they might introduce what form they then pleas'd; and without that occasion, the virtue of their mind had been extinguish'd; and without that virtue,

the occasion had been offer'd in vain. It was then necessary
for Moses to find the people of Israel slaves in Ægypt, and
oppress'd by the Ægyptians, to the end that they to get out
of their thraldome, should be willing to follow him. It was fit
that Romulus should not be kept in Albia, but expos'd presently after his birth, that he might become King of Rome, and
founder of that City. There was need that Cyrus should find
the Persians discontented with the Medes government, and
the Medes delicate and effeminate through their long peace.
Theseus could not make proof his virtue, had not he found
the Athenians dispers'd. These occasions therefore made
these men happy, and their excellent virtue made the occasion be taken notice of, whereby their country became eno-
bled, and exceeding fortunate. They, who by virtuous ways,
like unto these, become Princes, attain the Principality with
difficulty, but hold it with much ease; and the difficulties
they find in gaining the Principality, arise partly from the
new orders and courses they are forc'd to bring in, to lay the
foundation of their State, and work their own security. And
it is to be consider'd, how there is not any thing harder to
take in hand, nor doubtful to succeed, nor more dangerous
to manage, than to be the chief in bringing in new orders; for
this Chief finds all those his enemies, that thrive upon the
old orders; and hath but luke warm defenders of all those
that would do well upon the new orders, which luke-warm
temper proceeds partly from fear of the opposers who have
the laws to their advantage; partly from the incredulity of
the men who truly believe not a new thing, unless there be
some certain proof given them thereof. Whereupon it arises,
that whensoever they that are adversaries, take the occasion to assayle, they do it factiously; and these others defend
but coolly, so that their whole party altogether runs a hazard. Therefore it is necessary, being we intend thoroughly to
discourse this part, to examine if these innovators stand of
themselves, or if they depend upon others; that is, if to bring
their work to effect, it be necessary they should entreat, or
be able to constrain; in the first case they always succeed ill,
and bring nothing to pass; but when they depend of them-

selves, and are able to force, then seldom it is that they haz-ard. Hence came it that all the prophets that were arm'd, prevail'd; but those that were unarm'd, were too weak: for besides what we have alledg'd, the nature of the people is changeable, and easy to be persuaded to a matter; but it is hard also to settle them in that perswasion. And therefore it behoves a man to be so provided, that when they believe no longer, he may be able to compel them thereto by force. Moses, Cyrus, Theseus, and Romulus would never have been able to cause their Laws to be obey'd, had they been disarm'd; as in our times it befell Fryer Jerome Savanarola, who perished in his new constitutions, when the multitude began not to believe him; neither had he the means to keep them firm, that had beleev'd; not to force beleefe in them that had not beleev'd him. Wherefore such men as these, in their proceedings find great difficulty, and all their dangers are in the way, and these they must surmount by their virtue; but having once master'd them, and beginning to be honored by all, when they have rooted those out that envi'd their digni-ties, they remain powerful, secure, honorable, and happy. To these choice examples, I will add one of less remark; but it shall hold some proportion with them, and this shall suffice me for all others of this kind, which is Hiero the Siracusan. He of a private man, became Prince of Siracusa, nor knew he any other aid of fortune than the occasion: for the Sir-acusans being oppress'd, made choice of him for their Cap-tain, whereupon he deserv'd to be made their Prince: and he was of such virtue even in his private fortune, that he who writes of him, sayes, he wanted nothing of reigning, but a Kingdom; this man extinguish'd all the old soldiery, ordaind the new; left the old alliances, entertained new; and as he had friendship, and soldiers that were his own, upon that ground he was able to build any edifice; so that he endured much trouble in gaining, and suffered but little in maintain-ing.

Of New Principalities, Gotten by Fortune, and Other Mens Forces

They who by fortune only become Princes of private men, with small pains attain to it, but have much ado to maintain themselves in it; and find no difficulty at all in the way, because they are carried thither with wings: but all the difficulties arise there, after they are plac'd in them. And of such sort are those who have an estate given them for money, by the favor of some one that grants it them: as it befell many in Greece, in the cities of Jonia, and Hellespont; where divers Princes were made by Darius, as well for his own safety as his glory; as also them that were made Emperors; who from private men by corrupting the soldiers, attained to the Empire. These subsist merely upon the will, and fortune of those that have advanced them; which are two voluble and unsteady things; and they neither know how, nor are able to continue in that dignity: they know not how, because unless it be a man of great understanding and virtue, it is not probable that he who hath always liv'd a private life, can know how to command: neither are they able, because they have not any forces that can be friendly or faithful to them. Moreover those States that suddenly fall into a mans hands, as all other things in nature that spring and grow quickly, cannot well have taken root, nor have made their correspondences so firm, but that the first storm that takes them, ruins them; in case these, who (as it is said) are thus on a sudden clambered up to be Princes, are not of that worth and virtue as to know how to prepare themselves to maintain that which chance hath cast into their bosoms, and can afterwards lay those foundations, which others have cast before they were Princes. For the one and the other of these ways about the attaining to be a Prince, by Virtue, or by Fortune, I will allege you two examples which have been in the days of our memory. These were Francis Sforza, and Cæesar Borgia; Francis by just means and with a great deal of virtue, of a private man got to be Duke of Millan; and that which with much pains he had gained, he kept with small ado. On the other side Cæesar Borgia (commonly termed Duke Valentine) got his state by his Fathers fortune, and with the same lost it; however that for his own part no pains was spar'd, nor any thing omitted, which by a discreet and valorous man ought to have been done, to fasten his roots in those Estates, which others armies or fortune had bestowed on him; for (as it was formerly said) he that lays not the foundations first, yet might be able by means of his extraordinary virtues to lay them afterwards, however it be with the great trouble of the architect, and danger of the edifice. If therefore we consider all the Dukes progresses, we may perceive how great foundations he had cast for his future power, which I judge a matter not superfluous to run over; because I should not well know, what better rules I might give to a new Prince, than the pattern of his actions; and however the courses he took, availd him not, yet was it not his fault, but it proceeded from an extraordinary and extreme malignity of fortune. Pope Alexander the sixth, desiring to make the Duke his son a great man, had a great many difficulties, present and future: first he saw no way there was whereby he might be able to make him Lord of any State, that was not the Churches; and if he turned to take that from the Church, he knew that the Duke of Milan, and the Venetians would never agree to it; for Faenza and Riminum were under the Venetians protection. Moreover, he saw that the armies of Italy, and those whereof in particular he might have been able to make some use, were in their hands, who ought to fear the Popes greatness; and therefore could not any ways rely upon them: being all in the Orsins and Colonies hands, and those of their faction. It was necessary then, that those matters thus appointed by them should be disturbed, and the States of Italy disordered, to be able safely to master part of them, which he then found easy to do, seeing the Venetians upon three considerations had used the means to bring the French men back again into Italy: which he not only did not withstand, but furthered, with a resolution of King Lewis his ancient marriage. The King then past into Italy with the Venetians aid, and Alexanders consent; nor was he sooner arrived in Milan, than the Pope had soldiers from him for the service of Romania, which was quickly yielded up to him upon the reputation of the Kings forces. The Duke then having made himself master of

Romania, and beaten the Colonies, desiring to hold it, and proceed forward, two things hindered him: the one, his own soldiers, which he thought were not true to him; the other, the French mens good wills; that is to say, he feared that the Princes soldiers, whereof he had served himself, would fail him, and not only hinder his conquest, but take from him what he had gotten; and that the King also would serve him the same turn. He had experience of the Orsini upon an occasion, when after the taking of Faenza he assaulted Bolonia, to which assault he saw them go very cold. And touching the King, he discovered his mind, when having taken the Dutchy of Urbin, he invaded Tuscany; from which action the King made him retire; whereupon the Duke resolved to depend no more upon fortune, and other mens armies. And the first thing he did, was, to weaken the Orsini, and Colonnies factions in Rome: for he gain'd all their adherents that were gentlemen, giving them large allowances, and honoring them according to their qualities with charges and governments; so that in a few months the good will they bare to the parties was quite extinguished, and wholly bent to the Duke. After this, he waited an occasion to root out the Orsini, having before dispersed those of the family of Colonnia, which fell out well to his hand; and he used it better. For the Orsini being too late aware, that the Dukes and the Churches greatness was their destruction, held a Council together in a dwelling house of theirs in the country adjoyning to Perusia. From thence grew the rebellion of Urbin, and the troubles of Romania, and many other dangers befell the Duke, which he overcame all with the help of the French: and having regained his reputation, trusting neither France, nor any foreign forces, to the end he might not be put to make trial of them again, he betook himself to his sleghts; and he knew so well to disguise his intention, that the Orsins, by the mediation of Paul Orsine, were reconciled to him, to whom the Duke was no way wanting in all manner of courtesies whereby to bring them into security, giving them rich garments, money, and horses, til their own simplicities led them all to Sinigallia, into his hands. These heads being then pluck'd off, and their partisans made his friends; the Duke had laid very good foundations, to build his own greatness on, having in his power all Romania with the Dutchy of Urbin, and gained the hearts of those people, by beginning to give them some relish of their well being. And because this part is worthy to be taken notice of, and to be imitated by others, I will not let it escape. The Duke, when he had taken Romania, finding it had been under the hands of poor Lords who had rather pillag'd their subjects, than chastis'd or amended them, giving them more cause of discord, than of peace and union, so that the whole country was fraught with robberies, quarrels, and other sorts of insolencies; thought the best way to reduce them to terms of pacification, and obedience to a Princely power, was, to give them some good government: and therefore he set over them one Remiro D'Orco, a cruel hasty man, to whom he gave an absolute power. This man in a very short time settled peace and union amongst them with very great reputation. Afterwards the Duke thought such excessive authority serv'd not so well to his purpose, and doubting it would grow odious, he erected a civil Judicature in the midst of the country, where one excellent Judge did Preside, and thither every City sent their Advocate: and because he knew the rigors past had bred some hatred against him, to purge the minds of those people, and to gain them wholly to himself, he purpos'd to shew, that if there was any cruelty used, it proceeded not from any order of his, but from the harsh disposition of his Officers. Whereupon laying hold on him, at this occasion, he caused his head to be struck off one morning early in the market place at Cesena, where he was left upon a gibbet, with a bloody sword by his side; the cruelty of which spectacle for a while satisfied and amaz'd those people. But to return from whence we have digressed: I say, that the Duke finding himself very strong, and in part out of doubt of the present dangers, because he was arm'd after his own manner, and had in some good measure suppress'd those forces, which, because of their vicinity, were able to annoy him, he wanted nothing else to go on with his Conquest, but the consideration of France: for he knew, that the

King, who now, though late, was advis'd of his error, would never suffer him: and hereupon he began to seek after new alliances, and to waver with France, when the French came towards Naples against the Spaniards, who then besieged Gagetta; and his design was only to be out of their danger, which had been effected for him, had Pope Alexander lived. And thus were his business carried touching his present estate. As for the future, he had reason to doubt lest the new successor to the Papacy would not be his friend, and would endeavor to take that from him that Alexander had bestowed on him; and he thought to provide for this foure ways: First by rooting out the races of all those Lords he had dispoyled, whereby to take those occasions from the Pope. Secondly, by gaining all the gentlemen of Rome, whereby he might be able with those to keep the Pope in some awe. Thirdly, to make the Colledge of Cardinals as much at his devotion as possibly might be. Fourthly, by making of so large Conquests, before the Popes death, as that he might be able of himself to withstand the first fury of his enemies. Three of these four at Pope Alexanders death he had effected, and the fourth he had near brought to a point. For of those Lords he had striped, he put to death as many as he could come at, and very few escap'd him: he gained him the Roman Gentlemen: and in the Colledge he had made a great faction. And touching his new Conquest, he had a design to become Lord of Tuscany. And he had possessed himself already of Perusia, and Pombin, and taken protection of Pisa: and so soon as he should have cast off his respect to France (which now he meant to hold no longer) being the French were now driven out of the Kingdom of Naples by the Spaniards, so that each of them was forc'd to buy his friendship at any terms; he was then to leap into Pisa. After this Lucca and Siena were presently to fall to him, partly for envy to the Florentines, and partly for fear. The Florentines had no way to escape him: all which, had it succeeded with him, as without question it had, the very same year that Alexander dy'd, he had made himself master of so great forces, and such reputation, that he would have been able to have stood upon his own bottom, without any dependence of fortune, or resting upon others helps, but only upon his own strength and valor. But Alexander dy'd five years after that he had begun to draw forth his sword: and left him settled only in the State of Romania, with all his other designs in the air, sick unto death, between two very strong armies of his enemies; and yet was there in this Duke such a spirit and courage; and he understood so well, how men are to be gained, and how to be lost, and so firm were the grounds he had laid in a short time, that, had he not had those armies upon his back, or had been in health, he would have carried through his purpose in spight of all opposition; and that the foundations he grounded upon were good, it appeared in that Romania held for him above a moneth, and he remained secure in Rome, though even at deaths door: and however the Baglioni, Vitelli, and Orsini came into Rome; yet found they none would take their parts against him. And this he was able to have effected, that if he could not have made him Pope whom be would, he could have hindered him that he would not should be Pope. But had he been in health when Alexander dy'd, every thing had gone easily with him; and he told me on that day that Julius the second was created Pope, that he had fore-thought on all that which could happen, in case his father chanc'd to dye, and for every thing provided its remedy, this only excepted, that he foresaw not that he should at the same time be brought unto deaths dore also. Having then collected all the Dukes actions, me thinks I could not well blame him, but rather (as I have here done) set him as a pattern to be followed by all those who by fortune and others armies have been exalted to an Empire. For he being of great courage, and having lofty designs, could not carry himself otherwise; and the only obstacle of his purposes was the brevity of Alexanders life, and his own sickness. Whoever therefore deems it necessary in his entrance into a new Principality, to secure himself of his enemies, and gain him friends, to overcome either by force or by cunning, to make himself beloved, or feared of his people, be followed and reverenced by his soldiers, to root out those that can, or owe the any hurt, to

change the ancient orders with new ways, to be severe, and
yet acceptable, magnanimous, and liberal; to extinguish the
unfaithful soldiery, and create new; to maintain to himself
the amities of Kings and Princes, so that they shall either
with favor benefit the, or be wary how to offend the; cannot
find more fresh and lively examples than the actions of this
man. He deserves to be found fault with all for the creation
of Julius the second, wherein an evil choice was made for
him: for, as it is said, not being able to make a Pope to his
mind, he could have withheld any one from being Pope; and
should never have consented that any one of those Cardinals
should have got the Papacy, whom he had ever done harm
to; or who having attained the Pontificate were likely to be
afraid of him: because men ordinarily do hurt either for fear,
or hatred. Those whom he had offended, were among others,
he who had the title of St. Peter ad Vincula, Colonna, St.
George, and Ascanius; all the others that were in possibility
of the Popedome, were such as might have feared him rather,
except the Cardinal of Roan, and the Spaniards; these by
reason of their alliance and obligation with him, the other
because of the power they had, having the Kingdom of France
on their party; wherefore the Duke above all things should
have created a Spaniard Pope, and in case he could not have
done that, he should have agreed that Roan should have
been, and not St. Peter ad Vincula. And whoever believes,
that with great personages new benefits blot on the remembrance of old injuries, is much deceiv'd. The Duke therefore
in this election, was the cause of his own ruin at last.

Till wee come to this seventh Chapter, I find not any thing
much blame-worthy, unless it be on ground he lays in the
second Chapter; whereupon he builds most of this Fabric,
viz. That Subjects must either be dallied or flattered with all,
or quite crushed. Whereby our Author advises his Prince to
support his authority with two Cardinall Virtues, Dissimula-
tion, and Cruelty. He considers not herein that the head is
but a member of the body, though the principall; and the
end of the parts is the good of the whole. And here he goes
against himself in the twenty sixth Chapter of his Rep. 1. 1

where he blames Philip of Macedon for such courses, terming them very cruel, and against all Christian manner of living; and that every man should refuse to be a King, and desire rather to live a private life, than to reign so much to the ruin of mankind. The life of Cæsar Borgia, which is here given as a pattern to new Princes, we shall find to have been nothing else but a cunning carriage of things so, that he might thereby first deceive and inveigle, and then suppress all those that could oppose or hinder his ambition. For if you run over his life, you shall see the Father Pope Alexander the sixth and him, both embarked for his advancement, wherein they engag'd the Papall authority, and reputation of Religion; for faith and conscience these men never knew, though they exacted it of others: there was never promise made, but it was only so far kept as served for advantage; Liberality was made use of: Clemency and Cruelty, all alike, as they might serve to work with their purposes. All was sacrific'd to ambition; no friendship could tie these men, nor any religion: and no marvel: for ambition made them forget both God and man. But see the end of all this cunning: though this Cæsar Borgia contrived all his business so warily, that our Author much commends him, and he had attained near the pitch of his hopes, and had provided for each misadventure could befall him its remedy; Policy showed itself short-sighted; for he foresaw not at the time of his Fathers death, he himself should be brought unto deaths door also. And me thinks this Example might have given occasion to our Author to confess, that surely there is a God that ruleth the earth. And many times God cuts off those cunning and mighty men in the height of their purposes, when they think they have near surmounted all dangers and difficulties. 'To the intent that the living may know, that the most high ruleth in the Kingdom of men, and giveth it to whomsoever he will, and setteth up over it the basest of men.' Daniel. 4. 17.

Concerning Those Who by Wicked Means
Have Attained to a Principality

But because a man becomes a Prince of a private man two

ways, which cannot wholly be attributed either to Fortune or
Virtue, I think not fit to let them passe me: howbeit the one
of them may be more largely discoursed upon, where the Republics are treated of. These are, when by some wicked and
unlawful means a man rises to the Principality; or when a
private person by the favour of his fellow Citizens becomes
Prince of his country. And speaking of the first manner, it
shall be made evident by two Examples, the one ancient, the
other modern, without entering otherwise into the justice or
merit of this part; for I take it that these are sufficient for any
body that is forc'd to follow them. Agathocles the Sicilian, not
of a private man only, but from a base and abject fortune, got
to be King of Siracusa. This man borne but of a Potter, continued always a wicked life throughout all the degrees of this
fortune: nevertheless he accompanied his lewdness with
such a courage and resolution, that applying himself to military Affairs, by the degrees thereof he attained to be Prætour
of Siracusa, and being settled in that degree, and having de-
termined that he would become Prince, and hold that by violence and without obligation to any other, which by consent
had been granted him: and to this purpose having had some
private intelligence touching his design with Amilcar the
Carthaginian, who was employed with his army in Sicily, one
morining gathered the people together and the Senate of Syr-
acusa, as if he had some what to advise with them of matters
belonging to the Commonwealth, and upon a sign given,
caused his soldiers to kill his Senatours, and the richest of
the people; who being slain, he usurp'd the Principality of
that City without any civil strife: and however he was twice
broken by the Carthaginians, and at last besieged, was able
not only to defend his own City, but leaving part of his own
army at the defence thereof, with the other invaded Affrique,
and in a short time freed Siracusa from the siege, and brought
the Carthaginians into extreme necessity, who were constrained to accord with him, be contented with the possession of Affrique, and quit Sicily to Agathocles. He then that
should consider the actions and valor of this man, would not
see any, or very few things to be attributed unto Fortune;

seeing that as is formerly said, not by any ones favour, but by the degrees of service in war with many sufferings and dangers, to which he had risen, he came to the Principality; and that he maintained afterwards with so many resolute and hazardous undertakings. Yet cannot this be term'd virtue or valor to slay his own Citizens, betray his friends, to be without faith, without pity, without religion, which ways are of force to gain dominion, but not glory: for if Agathocles his valor be well weighed, in his entering upon, and coming off from dangers, and the greatness of his courage, in supporting and mastering of adversities, no man can see why he should be thought any way inferiour even to the ablest Captaines. Notwithstanding his beastly cruelty and inhumanity with innumerable wickedness, allow not that he should be celebrated among the most excellent men. That cannot then be attributed to Fortune or Virtue, which without the one or the other was attained to by him. In our days, while Alexander the sixth held the sea, Oliverotte of Fermo, who some few years before had been left young by his parents, was brought up under the care of an uncle of his on the mothers side, called John Foliani, and in the beginning of his youth given, by him to serve in the wars under Paulo Vitelli: to the end that being well instructed in that discipline, he might rise to some worthy degree in the wars. Afterwards when Paulo was dead, he served under Vitellozzo his brother, and in very short time, being ingenious, of a good personage, and brave courage, he became one of the prime men among the troops he served in: but thinking it but servile to depend upon another, he plotted by the aid of some Citizens of Fermo (who lik'd rather the thraldome of their City than the liberty of it) and by the favour of the Vitelli, to make himself master of Fermo; and writ to John Foliani, that having been many years from home, he had a mind to come and see him and the City, and in some part take notice of his own patrimony; and because he had not employed himself but to purchase honour, to the end his Citizens might perceive, that he had not vainly spent his time, he had a desire to come in good equipage and accompanied with a hundred horse of his friends and servants; and he entreated him that he would be pleased so to take order, that he might be honourably received by the inhabitants of Fermo, which turned as well to his honor that was his uncle, as his that was the nephew. In this, John failed not in any office of courtesy due to his nephew: and caused him to be well received by them of Fermo, and lodged him in his own house: where having passed some days, and staid to put in order somewhat that was necessary for his intended villainy, he made a very solemne feast, whether he invited John Foliani, and all the prime men of Fermo: and when all their chear was ended, and all their other entertainments, as in such feasts it is customary, Oliverotto of purpose mov'd some grave discourses; speaking of the greatness of Pope Alexander, and Cæsar his son, and their undertakings; where unto John and the others making answer, he of a sudden stood up, saying, that those were things to be spoken of in a more secret place, and so retir'd into a chamber, whether John and all the other Citizens followed him; nor were they sooner set down there, than from some secret place therein camp forth diverse soldiers, who slew John and all the others: after which homicide Oliverotto got a horsebacke and ravaged the whole town, and besieged the supreme Magistrate in the palace, so that for fear they were all constrained to obey him, and to settle a government, whereof he made himself Prince; and they being all dead who, had they been discontented with him, could have hurt him; he strengthened himself with new civil and military orders, so that in the space of a year that he held the Principality, he was not only secure in the City of Fermo, but became fearful to all his neighbours; and the conquest of him would have prov'd difficult, as that of Agathocles, had he not let himself been deceived by Cæsar Borgia, when at Sinigallia, as before was said, he took the Orsini and Vitelli: where he also being taken a year after he had committed the parricide, was strangled together with Vitellozzo (whom he had had for master both of his virtues and vices.) Some man might doubt from whence it should proceed, that Agathocles, and such like, after many treacheries and cruelties, could possibly live long secure in his own country, and defend himself from his foreign enemies, and that never any of his own Citizens conspir'd against him, seeing that by means of cruelty, many others have never been able even in peaceable times to maintain their States, much less in the doubtful times of war. I believe that this proceeds from the well, or ill using of those cruelties: they may be termed well used (if it be lawful to say well of evil) that are put in practice only once of necessity for securities sake, not insisting therein afterwards; but there is use made of them for the subjects profit, as much as may be. But those that are ill used, are such as though they be but few in the beginning, yet they multiply rather in time, than diminish. They that take that first way, may with the help of God, and mens care, find some remedy for their State, as Agathocles did: for the others, it is impossible they should continue. Whereupon it is to be noted, that in the laying hold of a State, the usurper thereof ought to run over and execute all his cruelties at once, that he be not forced often to return to them, and that he may be able, by not renewing of them, to give men some security, and gain their affections by doing them some courtesies. He that carries it otherwise, either for fearfulness, or upon evil advice, is always constrained to hold his sword drawn in his hand; nor ever can he rely upon his subjects, there being no possibility for them, because of his daily and continual injuries, to live in any safety: for his injuries should be done altogether, that being seldom tasted, they might less offend; his favours should be bestowd by little, and little to the end they might keep their taste the better; and above all things a Prince must live with his subjects in such sort, that no accident either of good or evil can make him vary: for necessity coming upon him by reason of adversities, thou hast not time given the to make advantage of thy cruelties; and the favours which then thou bestowest, will little help the, being taken as if they came from the perforce, and so yield no return of thanks.

Of the Civil Principality

But coming to the other part, when a principal Citizen, not

by villainy, or any other insufferable violence, but by the favour of his fellow-citizens becomes Prince of his native country: which we may terme a Civil Principality; nor to attain
hereunto is Virtue wholly or Fortune wholly necessary, but
rather a fortunate cunning: I say, this Principality is climb'd
up to, either by the peoples help, or the great mens. For, in
every City we finde these two humours differ; and they spring
from this, that the people desire not to be commanded nor
oppressed by the great ones, and the great ones are desirous
to command and oppresse the people: and from these two
several appetites, arise in the City one of these three effects,
either a Principality, or Liberty, or Tumultuary licentiousnesse. The Principality is caused either by the people, or the
great ones, according as the one or other of these factions
have the occasion offered; for the great ones seeing themselves not able to resist the people, begin to turn the whole
reputation to one among them, and make him Prince, whereby they may under his shadow vent their spleens. The people
also, not being able to support the great mens insolencies,
converting the whole reputation to one man, create him their
Prince, to be protected by his authority. He that comes to
the Principality by the assistance of the great ones, subsists
with more difficulty, than he that attains to it by the peoples
favour; for he being made Prince, hath many about him, who
account themselves his equals, and therefore cannot dispose
nor command them at his pleasure. But he that gains the
Principality by the peoples favor, finds himself alone in his
throne, and hath none or very few near him that are not very
supple to beend: besides this, the great ones cannot upon
easy terms be satisfied, or without doing of wrong to others,
where as a small matter contents the people: for the end
which the people propound to themselves, is more honest
than that of the great men, these desiring to oppress, they
only not to be oppressed. To this may be added also, that
the Prince which is the peoples enemy, can never well secure
himself of them, because of their multitude; well may he be
sure of the Nobles, they being but a few. The worst that a
Prince can look for of the people become his enemy, is to be

abandoned by them: but when the great ones once grow his
enemies, he is not only to fear their abandoning of him, but
their making of a party against him also: for there being in
them more forecast and craft, they always take time by the
forelocks whereby to save themselves, and seek credit with
him who they hope shall get the mastery. The Prince likewise
is necessitated always to live with the same people, but can
doe well enough without the same great men; he being able
to create new ones, and destroy them again every day, and
to take from them, and give them credit as he pleases: and to
clear this part, I say, that great men ought to be considered
two ways principally, that is, if they take thy proceedings so
much to heart, as to engage their fortunes wholly in thine,
in case they lye not always catching at spoil, they ought to
be well honourd and esteem'd: those that bind themselves
not to thy fortune, are to be considered also two ways; either they doe it for lack of courage, and naturall want of
spirit, and then shouldst thou serve thy self of them, and
of them especially that are men of good advice; for if thy
Affairs prosper, thou dost thy self honour thereby; if crost,
thou needst not fear them: but when they oblige not themselves to the of purpose, and upon occasion of ambition, it
is a signe they think more of themselves than of the: and of
these the Prince ought to beware, and account of them as
his discovered enemies: for always in thy adversity they will
give a hand too to ruin the. Therefore ought he that comes
to be Prince by the peoples favour, keep them his friends:
which he may easily doe, they desiring only to live free from
oppression: but he that becomes Prince by the great mens
favour, against the will of the people, ought above all things
to gain the people to him, which he may easily effect, when
he takes upon him their protection: And because men when
they find good, where they look for evil, are thereby more
endeared to their benefactor, therefore grows the people so
pliant in their subjection to him, as if by their favours he had
attained his dignity. And the Prince is able to gain them to
his side by many ways, which because they vary according to
the subject, no certain rule can be given thereupon; wherefore

we shall let them passe I will only conclude, that it is necessary for a Prince to have the people his friend; otherwise in
his adversities he hath no helpe. Nabis Prince of the Spartans
supported the siege of all Greece, and an exceeding victorious
army of the Romans, and against those defended his native
country and State, and this suffic'd him alone, that as the
danger came upon him, he secur'd himself of a fewer; whereas
if the people had been his enemy, this had nothing availd him.
And let no man think to overthrow this my opinion with that
common proverb, that He who relies upon the people, lays his
foundation in the dirt; for that is true where a private Citizen grounds upon them, making his account that the people
shall free him, when either his enemies or the Magistrates oppress him: In this case he should find himself often deceiv'd,
as it befell the Gracchyes in Rome, and in Florence George
Scali: but he being a Prince that grounds thereupon, who can
command, and is a man of courage, who hath his wits about
him in his adversities, and wants not other preparations, and
holds together the whole multitude animated with his valor
and orders, shall not prove deceiv'd by them, and shall find
he hath laid good foundations. These Principalities are wont
to be upon the point of falling when they go about to skip from
the civil order to the absolute: for these Princes either command of themselves, or by the Magistrate; in this last case
their State is more weak and dangerous, because they stand
wholly at the will and pleasure of these Citizens, who then are
set over the Magistrates, who especially in adverse times are
able with facility to take their State from them either by rising
up against them, or by not obeying them; and then the Prince
is not at hand in those dangers to take the absolute authority
upon him: for the Citizens and subjects that are accustomed
to receive the commands from the Magistrates, are not like
in those fractions to obey his: and in doubtful times he shall
always have greatest penury of whom he may trust; for such
a Prince cannot ground upon that which he sees in peaceable
times, when the Citizens have need of the State; for then every
one runs, and every one promises, and every one will venture
his life for him, where there is no danger near; but in times of

hazard, when the State hath need of Citizens, there are but few of them then, and so much the more is this experience dangerous, in that it can be but once made. Therefore a prudent Prince ought to devise a way whereby his Citizens always and in any case and quality of time may have need of his government, and they shall always after prove faithful to him.

In What Manner the Forces of All Principalities Ought to Be Measured

It is requisite in examining the quality of those Principalities, to have another consideration of them, that is, if a Prince have such dominions, that he is able in case of necessity to subsist of himself, or else whether he hath always need of another to defend him. And to clear this point the better, I judge them able to stand of themselves, who are of power either for their multitudes of men, or quantity of money, to bring into the field a compleat army, and joyn battle with whoever comes to assail them: and so I think those always to stand in need of others help, who are not able to appear in the field against the enemy, but are forc'd to retire within their walls and guard them. Touching the first case, we have treated already, and shall add somewhat thereto as occasion shall require. In the second case, we cannot say other, save only to encourage such Princes to fortify and guard their own Capital city, and of the country about, not to hold much account; and whoever shall have well fortified that town, and touching other matters of governments shall have behaved himself towards his subjects, as hath been formerly said, and hereafter shall be, shall never be assailed but with great regard; for men willingly undertake not enterprises, where they see difficulty to work them through; nor can much facility be there found, where one assails him, who hath his town strong and wel guarded, and is not hated of his people. The cities of Germany are very free; they have but very little of the country about them belonging to them; and they obey the Emperor, when they please, and they stand not in fear, neither of him nor any other Potentate about them: for they are in such a manner fortified, that every one thinks the

siege of any of them would prove hard and tedious: for all
of them have ditches, and rampires, and good store of Artil-
lery, and always have their public cellars well provided with
meat and drink and firing for a year: besides this, whereby
to feed the common people, and without any loss to the public, they have always in common whereby they are able for a
year to employ them in the labor of those trades that are the
sinews and the life of that city, and of that industry whereby
the commons ordinarily supported themselves: they hold up
also the military exercises in repute, and hereupon have they
many orders to maintain them. A Prince then that is master
of a good strong city, and causeth not himself to be hated,
cannot be assaulted; and in case he were, he that should
assail him, would be fain to quit him with shame: for the affairs of the world are so various, that it is almost impossible
that an army can lie encamped before a town for the space
of a whole year: and if any should reply, that the people having their possessions abroad, in case they should see them
a fire, would not have patience, and the tedious siege and
their love to themselves would make them forget their Prince:
I answer that a Prince puissant and courageous, will easily
master those difficulties, now giving his subjects hope, that
the mischief will not be of durance; sometimes affright them
with the cruelty of their enemies, and other whiles cunningly
securing himself of those whom he thinks too forward to run
to the enemy. Besides this by ordinary reason the enemy
should burn and waste their country, upon his arrival, and
at those times while mens minds are yet warm, and resolute in their defence: and therefore so much the less ought
a Prince doubt: for after some few days, that their courage
grow cool, the damages are all done, and mischiefs received,
and there is no help for it, and then have they more occasion to cleave faster to their Prince, thinking he is now more
bound to them, their houses having for his defence been
fired, and their possessions wasted; and mens nature is as
well to hold themselves oblig'd for the kindnesses they do,
as for those they receive; whereupon if all be well weigh'd, a
wise Prince shall not find much difficulty to keep sure and

true to him his Citizens hearts at the beginning and latter end of the siege, when he hath no want of provision for food and ammunition.

Concerning Ecclesiastical Principalities

There remains now only that we treat of the Ecclesiastical Principalities, about which all the difficulties are before they are gotten: for they are attained to either by virtue, or Fortune; and without the one or the other they are held: for they are maintained by orders inveterated in the religion, all which are so powerful and of such nature, that they maintain their Princes in their dominions in what manner soever they proceed and live. These only have an Estate and defend it not; have subjects and govern them not; and yet their States because undefended, are not taken from them; nor their subjects, though not govern'd, care not, think not, neither are able to align themselves from them. These Principalities then are only happy and secure: but they being sustained by superior causes, whereunto humane understanding reaches not, I will not meddle with them: for being set up and maintained by God, it would be the part of a presumptuous and rash man to enter into discourse of them. Yet if any man should ask me whence it proceeds, that the Church in temporal power hath attained to such greatness, seeing that till the time of Alexander the sixth, the Italian Potentates, and not only they who are entitled the potentates, but every Baron and Lord though of the meanst condition in regard of the temporality, made but small account of it; and now a King of France trembles at the power thereof; and it hath been able to drive him out of Italy, and ruin the Venetians; and however this be well known, me thinks it is not superstitious in some part to recall it to memory. Before that Charles King of France past into Italy, this country was under the rule of the Pope, Venetians, the King of Naples, the Duke of Milan, and the Florentines. These Potentates took two things principally to their care; the one, that no foreigner should invade Italy; the other that no one of them should enlarge their State. They, against whom this care was most taken, were the Pope and the Venetians; and to restrain the Venetians, there needed the union of all the rest, as it was in the defence of Ferrara; and to keep the Pope low, they served themselves of the Barons of Rome, who being divided into two factions, the Orsini and Colonnesi, there was always occasion of offence between them, who standing ready with their armies in hand in the view of the Pope, held the Pope-dome weak and feeble: and however sometimes there arose a couragious Pope, as was Sextus; yet either his fortune, or his wisdom was not able to free him of these incommodities, and the brevity of their lives was the cause thereof; for in ten years, which time, one with another, Popes ordinarily liv'd, with much ado could they bring low one of the factions. And if, as we may say, one had near put out the Colonnesi, there arose another enemy to the Orsini, who made them grow again, so that there was never time quite to root them out. This then was the cause, why the Popes temporal power was of small esteem in Italy; there arose afterwards Pope Alexander the sixth, who of all the Popes that ever were, shewed what a Pope was able to do with money and forces: and he effected, by means of his instrument, Duke Valentine, and by the occasion of the French mens passage, all those things which I have formerly discoursed upon in the Dukes actions: and however his purpose was nothing at all to enlarge the Church dominions, but to make the Duke great; yet what he did, turned to the Churches advantage, which after his death when the Duke was taken away, was the heir of all his pains. Afterwards succeeded Pope Julius, and found the Church great, having all Romania, and all the Barons of Rome being quite rooted out, and by Alexanders persecutions, all their factions worn down; he found also the way open for the heaping up of moneys, never practised before Alexanders time; which things Julius not only follow'd, but augmented; and thought to make himself master of Bolonia, and extinguish the Venetians, and chase the French men out of Italy: and these designs of his prov'd all lucky to him, and so much the more to his praise in that he did all for the good of the Church, and in no private regard: he kept also

the factions of the Orsins and Colonnesi, in the same State
he found them: and though there were among them some
head whereby to cause an alteration; yet two things have
held them quiet; the one the power of the Church, which
somewhat affrights them; the other because they have no
Cardinals of their factions, who are the primary causes of all
the troubles amongst them: nor shall these parties ever be
at rest, while they have Cardinals; because they nourish the
factions both in Rome, and abroad; and the Barons then are
forced to undertake the defence of them: and thus from the
Prelates ambitions arise the discords and tumults among the
Barons. And now hath Pope Leo his Holiness found the Popedome exceeding puissant, of whom it is hoped, that if they
amplified it by armies, he by his goodness, and infinite other
virtues, will much more advantage and dignify it.

How Many Sorts of Military Discipline
There Are and Touching Mercenary Soldiers

Having treated particularly of the qualities of those Principalities, which in the beginning I propounded to discourse
upon, and considered in some part the reasons of their well
and ill being, and showed the ways whereby many have
sought to gain, and hold them, it remains now that I speak
in general of the offences and defences, that may chance in
each of the forenamed. We have formerly said that it is necessary for a Prince to have good foundations laid; otherwise
it must needs be that he go to wrack. The Principal foundations that all States have, as well new, as old, or mixt, are
good laws, and good armies; and because there cannot be
good laws, where there are not good armies; and where there
are good armies, there must needs be good laws, I will omit
to discourse of the laws, and speak of armies. I say then that
the armies, wherewithal a Prince defends his State, either
are his own, or mercenary, or auxiliary, or mixt. Those that
are mercenary and auxiliar, are unprofitable, and dangerous, and if any one holds his State founded upon mercenary
armies, he shall never be quiet, nor secure, because they are
never well united, ambitious, and without discipline, treach-

erous, among their friends stour, among their enemies cowardly; they have no fear of God, nor keep any faith with men; and so long only defer they the doing of mischief, till the enemy comes to assail the; and in time of peace thou art despoyled by them, in war by thy enemies: the reason hereof is, because they have no other love, nor other cause to keep them in the field, but only a small stipend, which is not of force to make them willing to hazard their lives for the: they are willing indeed to be thy soldiers, till thou goest to fight; but then they fly, or run away; which thing would cost me but small pains to perswade; for the ruin of Italy hath not had any other cause now a days, than for that it hath these many years rely'd upon mercenary armies; which a good while since perhaps may have done some man some service, and among themselves they may have been thought valiant: but so soon as any foreign enemy appeared, they quickly shewed what they were. Whereupon Charles the King of France, without opposition, made himself master of all Italy: and he that said, that the causes thereof were our faults, said true; but these were not those they believed, but what I have told; and because they were the Princes faults, they also have suffered the punishment. I will fuller shew the infelicity of these armies. The mercenary Captains are either very able men, or not: if they be, thou canst not repose any trust in them: for they will always aspire unto their own proper advancements, either by suppressing of the that art their Lord, or by suppressing of some one else quite out of thy purpose: but if the Captain be not valorous, he ordinarily ruins the: and in case it be answered, that whoever shall have his armies in his hands, whether mercenary or not, will do so: I would reply, that armies are to be employed either by a Prince, or Common-wealth. The Prince ought to go in person, and perform the office of a commander: the Republic is to send forth her Citizens: and when she sends forth one that proves not of abilities, she ought to change him then; and when he does prove valorous, to bridle him so by the laws, that he exceed not his commission. And by experience we see, that Princes and Republiques of themselves alone, make very great conquests; but that mercenary armies never do other than harm; and more hardly falls a Republic armed with her own armies under the obedience of one of her own Citizens, than one that is armed by foreign armies. Rome and Sparta subsisted many ages armed and free. The Swissrs are exceedingly well armed, and yet very free. Touching mercenary armies that were of old, we have an example of the Carthagians, who near upon were oppress'd by their own mercenary soldiers, when the first war with the Romans was finished; however the Carthagians had their own Citizens for their Captains. Philip of Macedon was made by the Thebans after Epaminondas his death, General of their Armies; and after the victory, he took from them liberty. The Milaneses when Duke Philip was dead, entertaind Francis Sforza into their pay against the Venetians, who having vanquished their enemy at Caravaggio, afterwards joyned with them, where by to usurp upon the Milaneses his Masters. Sforza his father, being in Joan the Queen of Naples pay, left her on a sudden disarmed; whereupon she, to save her Kingdom, was constrained to cast her self into the King of Arrragon's bosome. And in case the Venetians and the Florentines have formerly augmented their State with these kind of armies, and their own Captains, and yet none of them have ever made themselves their Princes, but rather defended them: I answer, that the Florentines in this case have had fortune much their friend: for of valorous Captains, which they might any way fear, some have not been victors, some have had opposition, and others have laid the aim of their ambitions another way. He who overcame not, was John Aouto, of whose faith there could no proof be made, being he vanquished not; but every one will acknowledge, that, had he vanquished, the Florentines were at his discretion. Sforza had always the Bracceschi for his adversaries, so that they were as a guard one upon another. Francis converted all his ambition against Lombardy. Braccio against the Church, and the Kingdom of Naples. But let us come to that which followed a while agoe. The Florentines made Paul Vitelli their General, a throughly advis'd man, and who from a private fortune had rose to very great reputation: had he taken Pisa, no man will deny but that the Florentines must have held fast with him; for had he been entertained in their enemies pay, they had no remedy; and they themselves holding of him, of force were to obey him. The Venetians, if we consider their proceedings, we shall see wrought both warily and gloriously, while themselves made war, which was before their undertakings by land, where the gentlemen with their own Commons in armies behav'd themselves bravely: but when they began to fight by land, they lost their valor, and follow'd the customs of Italy; and in the beginning of their enlargement by land, because they had not much territory, and yet were of great reputation, they had not much cause to fear their Captains; but as they began to extend their bounds, which was under their Commander Carminiola, they had a taste of this error: for perceiving he was exceeding valorous, having under his conduct beaten the Duke of Milan; and knowing on the other side, how he was cold in the war, they judg'd that they could not make any great conquest with him; and because they neither would, nor could cashier him, that they might not lose what they had gotten, they were forced for their own safeties to put him to death. Since they have had for their General Bartholomew of Berganio, Robert of St. Severin, the Count of Petilian, and such like: whereby they were to fear their losses, as well as to hope for gain: as it fell out afterwards at Vayla, where in one day they lost that, which with so much pains they had gotten in eight hundred years: for from these kind of armies grow slack and slow and weak gains; but sudden and wonderful losses: And because I am now come with these examples into Italy, which now these many years, have been governed by mercenary armies, I will search deeper into them, to the end that their course and progress being better discovered, they may be the better amended. You have to understand, that so soon as in these later times the yolk of the Italian Empire began to be shaken off, and the Pope had gotten reputation in the temporality, Italy was divided into several States: for many of the great cities took armies against their Nobility; who under the Emperors protection had held them in oppression; and the Pope favored these, whereby he might get himself reputation, in the temporality; of many others, their Citizens became Princes, so that hereupon Italy being come into the Churches hands as it were, and some few Republics, those Priests and Citizens not accustomed to the use of armies, began to take strangers to their pay. The first that gave reputation to these soldiers was Alberick of Como in Romania. From his discipline among others descended Brachio and Sforza, who in their time were the arbitres of Italy; after these followed all others, who even till our days have commanded the armies of Italy; and the success of their valor hath been, that it was overrun by Charles, pillaged by Lewis, forc'd by Ferdinand, and disgrac'd by the Swissrs. The order which they have held, hath been, first whereby to give reputation to their own armies to take away the credit of the Infantry. This they did, because they having no State of their own, but living upon their industry, their few foot gave them no reputation, and many they were not able to maintain; whereupon they reduc'd themselves to cavalry, and so with a supportable number they were entertained and honored: and matters were brought to such terms, that in an army of twenty thousand soldiers you should not find two thousand foot. They had moreover used all industry to free themselves and their soldiers of all pains and fear, in their skirmishes, not killing, but taking one another prisoners, and without ransom for their freedom; they repaired not all to their tents by night, nor made palizado or trench thereabout, nor lay in the field in the summer: and all these things were thus contrived and agreed of among them in their military orders, whereby (as is said) to avoid pains and dangers, insomuch as they have brought Italy into slavery and disgrace.

Of Auxiliary Soldiers, Mixt, and Native

The Auxiliary forces, being the other kind of unprofitable armies, are, when any puissant one is called in, who with his forces comes to assist and defend the; such as in these later times did Pope Julius use, who having seen the evil proof of his mercenary soldiers in the enterprise of Ferrara, applied himself to the Auxiliaries, and agreed with Ferdinand King of Spain, that with his Forces he should aid him. These armies may be profitable and advantageous for themselves; but for him that calls them in, hurtful; because in losing, thou art left defeated; and conquering, thou becomest their prisoner. And however that of these examples the ancient stories are full fraught; yet will I not part from this of Pope Julius the second, which is as yet fresh: whose course could not have been more inconsiderate, for the desire he had to get Ferrara, putting himself wholly into strangers hands: but his good fortune caused another cause to arise, that hindered him from receiving the fruit of his evil choice; for his Auxiliaries being broken at Ravenna, and the Swissrs thereupon arriving, who put the Conquerors to flight beyond all opinion, even their own and others, he chanced not to remain his enemies prisoner, they being put to flight, nor prisoner to his Auxiliaries, having vanquished by other forces than theirs. The Florentines being wholly disarmed, brought ten thousand French to Pisa for to take it: by which course they ran more hazard, than in any time of their troubles. The Emperor of Constantinople, to oppress his neighbors, brought into Greece ten thousand Turks, who when the war was ended, could not be got out thence, which was the beginning of Greeces servitude under the Infidels. He then that will in no case be able to overcome, let him serve himself of these armies; for they are much more dangerous than the mercenaries; for by those thy ruin is more suddenly executed; for they are all united, and all bent to the obedience of another. But for the mercenaries to hurt the, when they have vanquished, there is no more need of time, and greater occasion, they not being all united in a body, and being found out and paid by the, wherein a third that thou mak'st their head, cannot suddenly gain so great authority, that he can endammage the. In some, in the mercenaries their sloth and laziness to fight is more dangerous: in the auxiliaries their valor. Wherefore a wise Prince hath always avoided these kind of armies, and betaken himself to his own, and desired rather to loss with his own, than conquer with another, accounting that not a true victory which was gotten with others armies. I will not doubt to alleadge Cæsar Borgia, and his actions. This Duke entered into Romania with auxiliarie armies, bringing with him all French soldiers: but afterwards not accounting those armies secure, bent himself to mercenaries, judging lesse danger to be in those, and tooke in pay the Orsini and the Vitelli, which afterwards in the proof of them, finding wavering, unfaithful, and dangerous, he extinguished, and betook himself to his own; and it may easily be perceiv'd what difference there is between the one and the other of these armies, considering the difference that was between the Dukes reputation, when he had the French men alone, and when he had the Orsini and Vitelli; but when he remaind with his own, and stood of himself, we shall find it was much augmented: nor ever was it of grate esteem, but when every one saw, that he wholly possessed his own armies. I thought not to have partd from the Italian examples of late memory; but that I must not let passe that of Hiero the Siracusan, being one of those I formerly nam'd. This man (as I said before) being made general of the Siracusans forces, knew presently that mercenary souldiery was nothing for their profit in that they were hirelings, as our Italians are; and finding no way either to hold, or cashier them made them all be cut to pieces, and afterwards waged war with his own men, and none others. I will also call to memory a figure of the old Testament serving just to this purpose. When David presented himself before Saul to goe to fight with Goliah the Philistins Champion, Saul to encourage him, clad him with his own armies, which David when he had them upon back, refused, saying, he was not able to make any proof of himself therein, and therefore would goe meet the enemy with his own sling and sword. In sum, others armies either fall from thy shoulders, or cumber or straighten the. Charls the seventh, Father of Lewis the eleventh, having by his good fortune and valor set France at liberty from the English, knew well this necessity of being arm'd with his own armies, and settled in his Kingdom the ordinances of men at armies, and infantry. Afterwards King Lewis his son abolished those of the infantry, and began to take the Swissrs to pay; which error follow'd by the others, is (as now indeed it appears) the cause of that Kingdoms dangers. For having given reputation to the Swissrs, they have rendered all their own armies contemptible; for this hath wholly ruined their foot, and oblig'd their men at armies to foreign armies: for being accustomed to serve with the Swissrs, they think they are not able to overcome without them. From whence it comes that the French are not of force against the Swissrs, and without them also against others they use not to adventure. Therefore are the French armies mixt, part mercenaries, and part natives, which armies are far better than the simple mercenaries or simple auxiliaries, and much inferiour to the natives; and let the said example suffice for that: for the Kingdom of France would have been unconquerable, if Charles his order had been augmented and maintained: but men in their small wisdom begin a thing, which then because it hath some favour of good, discovers not the poison that lurks thereunder, as I before said of the hectic fevers. Wherefore that Prince which perceives not mischiefs, but as they grow up, is not truly wise; and this is given but to few: and if we consider the first ruin of the Romane Empire, we shall find it was from taking the Goths first into their pay; for from that beginning the forces of the Romane Empire began to grow weak, and all the valor that was taken hence was given to them. I conclude then that without having armies of their own, no Principality can be secure, or rather is wholly oblig'd to fortune, not having valor to shelter it in adversity. And it was always the opinion and saying of wise men, that nothing is so weak and unsettled, as is the reputation of power not founded upon ones own proper forces: which are those that are composed of thy subjects, or Citizens, or servants; all the rest are mercenary or auxiliary; and the manner how to order those well, is easy to find out, if those orders above nam'd by me, shall be but run over, and if it shall be but consider'd, how Philip Alexander the Great his Father, and in what manner many Republics and Princes have armed and appointed themselves, to which appointments I refer my self wholly.

What Belongs to the Prince Touching Military Discipline

A prince then ought to have no other aim, nor other thought, nor take any thing else for his proper art, but war, and the orders and discipline thereof: for that is the sole art which belongs to him that commands, and is of so great excellency, that not only those that are borne Princes, it maintains so; but many times raises men from a private fortune to that dignity. And it is seen by the contrary, that when Princes have given themselves more to their delights, than to the wars, they have lost their States; and the first cause that makes the lose it, is the neglect of that art; and the cause that makes the gain it, is that thou art experienc'd and approved in that art. Francis Sforza by being a man at armies, of a private man became Duke of Milan; and his sons by excusing themselves of the troubles and pains belonging to those employments of Princes, became private men. For among other mischiefs thy neglect of armies brings upon the, it causes the to be condemned, which is one of those disgraces, from which a Prince ought to keep himself, as hereafter shall be said: for from one that is disarmed to one that is armed there is no proportion; and reason will not, that he who is in armies, should willingly yield obedience to him that is unfurnished of them, and that he that is disarmed should be in security among his armed vassals; for there being disdain in the one, and suspicion in the other, it is impossible these should ever well cooperate. And therefore a Prince who is quite unexperienced in matter of war, besides the other infelicities belonging to him, as is said, cannot be had in any esteem among his soldiers, nor yet trust in them. Wherefore he ought never to neglect the practice of the art of war, and in time of peace should he exercise it more than in the war; which he may be able to doe two ways; the one practically, and in his labours and recreations of his body, the other theoretically. And touching the practical part, he ought besides the keeping of his own subjects well trained up in the discipline and exercise of armies, give himself much to the chase, whereby to accustom his body to pains, and partly to understand the manner of situations, and to know how the mountains arise,

which way the valleys open themselves, and how the planes
are distended flat abroad, and to conceive well the nature of
the rivers, and marshy ground, and herein to bestow very
much care, which knowledge is profitable in two kinds: first
he learns thereby to know his own country, and is the better
enabled to understand the defence thereof, and afterwards
by means of this knowledge and experience in these situations, easily comprehends any other situation, which a new
he hath need to view, for the little hillocks, valleys, planes,
rivers, and marshy places. For example, they in Tuscany are
like unto those of other countries: so that from the knowledge of the site of one country, it is easy to attain to know
that of others. And that Prince that wants this skill, fails of
the principal part a Commander should be furnished with;
for this shows the way how to discover the enemy, to pitch
the camp, to lead their armies, to order their battles, and
also to besiege a town at thy best advantage, Philopomenes
Prince of the Achayans, among other praises Writers give
him, they say, that in time of peace, he thought not upon
any thing so much as the practise of war; and whensoever
he was abroad in the field to disport himself with his friends,
would often stand still, and discourse with them, in case the
enemies were upon the top of that hill, and we here with our
army, whether of us two should have the advantage, and
how might we safely go to find them, keeping still our orders;
and if we would retire our selves, what course should we
take if they retir'd, how should we follow them? and thus on
the way, propounded them all such accidents could befall in
any army; would hear their opinions, and tell his own, and
confirm it by argument; so that by his continual thought
hereupon, when ever he led any army no chance could happen, for which he had not a remedy. But touching the exercise of the mind, a Prince ought to read Histories, and in
them consider the actions of the worthiest men, mark how
they have behav'd themselves in the wars, examine the occasions of their victories, and their losses; whereby they may
be able to avoid these, and obtain those; and above all, doe
as formerly some excellent man hath done, who hath taken

upon him to imitate, if any one that hath gone before him
hath left his memory glorious; the course he took, and kept
always near unto him the remembrances of his actions and
worthy deeds: as it is said, that Alexander the great imitated
Achilles; Cæsar Alexander, and Scipio Cyrus. And whoever
reads the life of Cyrus, written by Xenophon, may easily perceive afterwards in Scipio's life how much glory his imitation
gained him, and how much Scipio did conform himself in
his chastity, affability, humanity, and liberality with those
things, that are written by Xenophon of Cyrus. Such like
ways ought a wise Prince to take, nor ever be idle in quiet
times, but by his pains then, as it were provide himself of
store, whereof he may make some use in his adversity, the
end that when the times change, he may be able to resist the
storms of his hard fortune.

Of Those Things, in Respect Whereof, Men, and Especially Princes, Are Praised, or Dispraised

It now remaines that we consider what the conditions of
a Prince ought to be, and his terms of government over his
subjects, and towards his friends. And because I know that
many have written hereupon; I doubt, lest I venturing also to
treat thereof, may be branded with presumption, especially
seeing I am like enough to deliver an opinion different from
others. But my intent being to write for the advantage of him
that understands me, I thought it fitter to follow the effectual
truth of the matter, than the imagination thereof; And many
Principalities and Republiques, have been in imagination,
which neither have been seen nor known to be indeed: for
there is such a distance between how men doe live, and how
men ought to live; that he who leaves that which is done, for
that which ought to be done, learns sooner his ruin than his
preservation; for that man who will profess honesty in all his
actions, must needs go to ruin among so many that are dishonest. Whereupon it is necessary for a Prince, desiring to
preserve himself, to be able to make use of that honestie, and
to lay it aside again, as need shall require. Passing by then

things that are only in imagination belonging to a Prince, to discourse upon those that are really true; I say that all men, whensoever mention is made of them, and especially Princes, because they are placed aloft in the view of all, are taken notice of for some of these qualities, which procure them either commendations or blame: and this is that some one is held liberal, some miserable, (miserable I say, nor covetous; for the covetous desire to have, though it were by rapine; but a miserable man is he, that too much for bears to make use of his own) some free givers, others extortioners; some cruel, others pitious; the one a Leaguebreaker, another faithful; the one effeminate and of small courage, the other fierce and courageous; the one courteous, the other proud; the one lascivious, the other chaste; the one of faire dealing, the other wily and crafty; the one hard, the other easy; the one grave, the other light; the one religious, the other incredulous, and such like. I know that every one will confess, it were exceedingly praise worthy for a Prince to be adored with all these above nam'd qualities that are good: but because this is not possible, nor doe humane conditions admit such perfection in virtues, it is necessary for him to be so discreet, that he know how to avoid the infamy of those vices which would thrust him out of his State; and if it be possible, beware of those also which are not able to remove him thence; but where it cannot be, let them passe with less regard. And yet, let him not stand much upon it, though he incur the infamy of those vices, without which he can very hardly save his State: for if all be thoroughly considered, some thing we shall find which will have the colour and very face of Virtue, and following them, they will lead the to thy destruction; whereas some others that shall as much seem vice, if we take the course they lead us, shall discover unto us the way to our safety and well-being.

The second blemish in this our Authours book, I find in his fifteenth Chapter: where he instructs his Prince to use such an ambidexterity as that he may serve himself either of virtue, or vice, according to his advantage, which in true pollicy is neither good in attaining the Principality nor in securing it when it is attained. For Politicks, presuppose Ethiques, which will never allow this rule: as that a man might make this small difference between virtue, and vice, that he may indifferently lay aside, or take up the one or the other, and put it in practise as best conduceth to the end he propounds himself. I doubt our Authour would have blamed Davids regard to Saul when 1 Sam. 24 in the cave he cut off the lap of Sauls garment, and spared his head; and afterwards in the 26 when he forbad Abishai to strike him as he lay sleeping. Worthy of a Princes consideration is that saying of Abigal to David 1 Sam. 25. 30.

'It shall come to passe when the Lord shall have done to my Lord according to all that he hath spoken concerning the, and shall have appointed the Ruler over Israel, that this shall be no grief to the, nor offence of heart unto my Lord, that thou hast forborne to shed blood, etc.'

For surely the conscience of this evil ground whereupon they have either built, or underpropped their tyranny, causes men, as well met us as spes in longum projicere, which sets them a work on further mischief.

Of Liberality, and Miserablenesse

Beginning then at the first of the above mentioned qualities, I say that it would be very well to be accounted liberal: nevertheless, liberality used in such a manner, as to make the be accounted so, wrongs the: for in case it be used virtuously, and as it ought to be, it shall never come to be taken notice of, so as to free the from the infamy of its contrary. And therefore for one to hold the name of liberal among men, it were needfull not to omit any sumptuous quality, insomuch that a Prince always so dispos'd, shall waste all his revenues, and at the end shall be forc'd, if he will still maintain that reputation of liberality, heavily to burden his subjects, and become a great exactor; and put in practise all those things that can be done to get mony: Which begins to make him hateful to his subjects, and fall into every ones contempt, growing necessitous: so that having with this liberality wrong'd many, and impartd of his bounty but to a few; he feels every first mischance, and runs a hazard of every first danger: Which he knowing, and desiring to withdraw himself from, incurs presently the disgrace of being termed miserable. A Prince therefore not being able to use this virtue of liberality, without his own damage, in such a sort, that it may be taken notice of, ought, if he be wise, not to regard the name of Miserable; for in time he shall always be esteemed the more liberal, seeing that by his parsimony his own revenues are sufficient for him; as also he can defend himself against whoever makes war against him, and can do some exploits without grieving his subjects: so that he comes to use his liberality to all those, from whom he takes nothing, who are infinite in number; and his miserableness towards those to whom he gives nothing, who are but a few. In our days we have not seen any, but those who have been held miserable, do any great matters; but the others all quite ruin'd. Pope Julius the second, however he serv'd himself of the name of Liberal, to get the Papacy, yet never intended he to continue it, to the end he might be able to make war against the King of France: and he made so many wars without imposing any extraordinary tax, because his long thrift supplied his large expenses. This present King of Spain could never have undertaken, nor gone through with so many exploits, had he been accounted liberal. Wherefore a Prince ought little to regard (that he may not be driven to pillage his subjects, that he may be able to defend himself, that he may not fall into poverty and contempt, that he be not forced to become an extortioner) though he incur the name of miserable; for this is one of those vices, which does not pluck him from his throne. And if any one should say, Cæsar by his liberality obtained the Empire, and many others (because they both were, and were esteemed liberal) attained to exceeding great dignities. I answer, either thou art already come to be a Prince, or thou art in the way to it; in the first case, this liberality is hurtful; in the second, it is necessary to be accounted so; and Cæsar was one of those that aspired to the Principality of Rome. But if after he had gotten it, he had survived, and not forborne those expenses, he would quite have ruined that Empire. And if any one should reply; many have been Princes, and with their armies have done great exploits, who have been held very liberal. I answer, either the Prince spends of his own and his subjects, or that which belongs to others: in the first, he ought to be sparing; in the second, he should not omit any part of liberality. And that Prince that goes abroad with his army, and feeds upon prey, and spoyle, and tributes, and hath the disposing of that which belongs to others, necessarily should use this liberality; otherwise would his soldiers never follow him; and of that which is neither thine, nor thy subjects, thou mayest well be a free giver, as were Cyrus, Cæsar and Alexander; for the spending of that which is anothers, takes not away thy reputation, but rather adds to it, only the wasting of that which is thine own hurts the; nor is there any thing consumes itself so much as liberality, which whilest thou usest, thou losest the means to make use of it, and becomest poor and abject; or to avoid this poverty, an extortioner and hateful person. And among all those things which a Prince ought to beware of is, to be despised, and odious; to one and the other of which, liberality brings the. Wherefore there is more discretion to hold the stile of Miserable, which begets an infamy without hatred, than to desire that of Liberal, whereby to incur the necessity of being thought an extortioner, which procures an infamy with hatred.

Of Cruelty, and Clemency, and Whether it Is Better to Be Belov'd, or Feared

Descending afterwards unto the other fore-alleged qualities, I say, that every Prince should desire to be held pitiful, and not cruel. Nevertheless ought he beware that he ill uses not this pity. Cæsar Borgia was accounted cruel, yet had his cruelty redrest the disorders in Romania, settled it in union, and restored it to peace, and fidelity: which, if it be well weighed, we shall see was an act of more pity, than that of the people of Florence, who to avoid the term of cruelty, suffered Pistoya to fall to destruction. Wherefore a Prince ought not to regard the infamy of cruelty, for to hold his subjects united and faithful: for by giving a very few proofs of himself the other way, he shall be held more pitiful than they, who through their too much pity, suffer disorders to follow, from whence arise murders and rapines: for these are wont to hurt an entire universality, whereas the executions practised by a Prince, hurt only some particular. And among all sorts of Princes, it is impossible for a new Prince to avoid the name of cruel, because all new States are full of dangers: whereupon Virgil by the mouth of Dido excuses the inhumanity of her Kingdom, saying,

Res dura et Regni novitas me talia cogunt Moliri et latè fines custode tenere.

My hard plight and new State force me to guard My confines all about with watch and ward.

Nevertheless ought he to be judicious in his giving belief to any thing, or moving himself thereat, nor make his people extremely afraid of him; but proceed in a moderate way with wisdom, and humanity, that his too much confidence make him not unwary, and his too much distrust intolerable; from hence arises a dispute, whether it is better to be belov'd or feared: I answer, a man would wish he might be the one and the other: but because hardly can they subsist both together, it is much safer to be feared, than be loved; being that one of the two must needs fail; for touching men, we may say this in general, they are unthankful, unconstant, dissemblers, they avoid dangers, and are covetous of gain; and whilest thou doest them good, they are wholly thine; their blood, their fortunes, lives and children are at thy service, as is said before, when the danger is remote; but when it approaches, they revolt. And that Prince who wholly relies upon their words, unfurnished of all other preparations, goes to wrack: for the friendships that are gotten with rewards, and not by the magnificence and worth of the mind, are dearly bought indeed; but they will neither keep long, nor serve well in time of need: and men do less regard to offend one that is supported by love, than by fear. For love is held by a certainty of obligation, which because men are mischievous, is broken upon any occasion of their own profit. But fear restrains with a dread of

punishment which never forsakes a man. Yet ought a Prince
cause himself to be belov'd in such a manner, that if he gains
not love, he may avoid hatred: for it may well stand together,
that a man may be feared and not hated; which shall never
fail, if he abstain from his subjects goods, and their wives;
and whensoever he should be forc'd to proceed against any
of their lives, do it when it is to be done upon a just cause,
and apparent conviction; but above all things forbear to lay
his hands on other mens goods; for men forget sooner the
death of their father, than the loss of their patrimony. Moreover the occasions of taking from men their goods, do never
fail: and always he that begins to live by rapine, finds occasion to lay hold upon other mens goods: but against mens
lives, they are seldom found, and sooner fail. But where a
Prince is abroad in the field with his army, and hath a multitude of soldiers under his government, then is it necessary
that he stands not much upon it, though he be termed cruel:
for unless he be so, he shall never have his soldiers live in
accord one with another, nor ever well disposed to any brave
piece of service. Among Hannibals actions of mervail, this is
reckoned for one, that having a very huge army, gathered out
of several nations, and all led to serve in a strange country,
there was never any dissention neither amongst themselves,
nor against their General, as well in their bad fortune as
their good. Which could not proceed from any thing else than
from that barbarous cruelty of his, which together with his
exceeding many virtues, rendered him to his soldiers both
venerable and terrible; without which, to that effect his other
virtues had served him to little purpose: and some writers
though not of the best advised, on one side admire these his
worthy actions, and on the other side, condemn the principal causes thereof. And that it is true, that his other virtues
would not have suffic'd him, we may consider in Scipio, the
rarest man not only in the days he liv'd, but even in the
memory of man; from whom his army rebel'd in Spain: which
grew only upon his too much clemency, which had given
way to his soldiers to become more licentious, than was well
tolerable by military discipline: for which he was reprov'd

by Fabius Maximus in the Senate, who termed him the corrupter of the Roman soldiery. The Locrensians having been destroyed by a Lieutenant of Scipio's, were never reveng'd by him, nor the insolence of that Lieutenant punisht; all this arising from his easy nature: so that one desiring to excuse him in the Senate, said, that there were many men knew better how to keep themselves from faults, than to correct the faults of other men: which disposition of his in time would have wrong'd Scipio's reputation and glory, had he therewith continu'd in his commands: but living under the government of the Senate, this quality of his that would have disgrac'd him not only was conceal'd, but prov'd to the advancement of his glory. I conclude then, returning to the purpose of being feared, and belov'd; insomuch as men love at their own pleasure, and to serve their own turn, and their fear depends upon the Princes pleasure, every wise Prince ought to ground upon that which is of himself, and not upon that which is of another: only this, he ought to use his best wits to avoid hatred, as was said.

In What Manner Princes Ought to Keep Their Words

How commendable in a Prince it is to keep his word, and live with integrity, not making use of cunning and subtlety, every one knows well: yet we see by experience in these our days, that those Princes have effected great matters, who have made small reckoning of keeping their words, and have known by their craft to turn and wind men about, and in the end, have overcome those who have grounded upon the truth. You must then know, there are two kinds of combating or fighting; the one by right of the laws, the other merely by force. That first way is proper to men, the other is also common to beasts: but because the first many times suffices not, there is a necessity to make recourse to the second; wherefore it behooves a Prince to know how to make good use of that part which belongs to a beast, as well as that which is proper to a man. This part hath been covertly shew'd to Princes by ancient writers; who say that Achilles and many others of those ancient Princes were intrusted to Chiron the Senator, to be brought up under his discipline: the moral of this, having for their teacher one that was half a beast and half a man, was nothing else, but that it was needful for a Prince to understand how to make his advantage of the one and the other nature, because neither could subsist without the other. A Prince then being necessitated to know how to make use of that part belonging to a beast, ought to serve himself of the conditions of the Fox and the Lion; for the Lion cannot keep himself from snares, nor the Fox defend himself against the Wolves. He had need then be a Fox, that he may beware of the snares, and a Lion that he may scare the wolves. Those that stand wholly upon the Lion, understand not well themselves. And therefore a wise Prince cannot, nor ought not keep his faith given when the observance thereof turns to disadvantage, and the occasions that made him promise, are past. For if men were all good, this rule would not be allowable; but being they are full of mischief, and would not make it good to the, neither art thou tied to keep it with them: nor shall a Prince ever want lawful occasions to give colour to this breach. Very many modern examples hereof might be alledg'd, wherein might be shewed how many pieces concluded, and how many promises made, have been violated and broken by the infidelity of Princes; and ordinarily things have best succeeded with him that hath been nearst the Fox in condition. But it is necessary to understand how to set a good colour upon this disposition, and to be able to fain and dissemble thoroughly; and men are so simple, and yield so much to the present necessities, that he who hath a mind to deceive, shall always find another that will be deceived. I will not conceal any one of the examples that have been of late. Alexander the sixth, never did any thing else than deceive men, and never meant otherwise, and always found whom to work upon; yet never was there man would protest more effectually, nor aver any thing with more solemn oaths, and observe them less than he; nevertheless, his cousenages all thriv'd well with him; for he knew how to play this part cunningly. Therefore is there no neces-

sity for a Prince to be endued with all above written qualities, but it behooveth well that he seem to be so; or rather I
will boldly say this, that having these qualities, and always
regulating himself by them, they are hurtful; but seeming to
have them, they are advantageous; as to seem pitiful, faithful, mild, religious, and of integrity, and indeed to be so; provided with all thou beast of such a composition, that if need
require to use the contrary, thou canst, and knowest how to
apply thy self thereto. And it suffices to conceive this, that a
Prince, and especially a new Prince, cannot observe all those
things, for which men are held good; he being often forc'd,
for the maintenance of his State, to do contrary to his faith,
charity, humanity, and religion: and therefore it behooves
him to have a mind so disposed, as to turn and take the
advantage of all winds and fortunes; and as formerly I said,
not forsake the good, while he can; but to know how to make
use of the evil upon necessity. A Prince then ought to have
a special care, that he never let fall any words, but what are
all season'd with the five above written qualities, and let him
seem to him that sees and hears him, all pity, all faith, all integrity, all humanity, all religion; nor is there any thing more
necessary for him to seem to have, than this last quality: for
all men in general judge thereof, rather by the sight, than by
the touch; for every man may come to the sight of him, few
come to the touch and feeling of him; every man may come to
see what thou seemest, few come to perceive and understand
what thou art; and those few dare not oppose the opinion of
many, who have the majesty of State to protect them: And in
all mens actions, especially those of Princes wherein there is
no judgement to appeal unto men, forbear to give their cen-
sures, till the events and ends of things. Let a Prince therefore take the surest courses he can to maintain his life and
State: the means shall always be thought honorable, and
commended by every one; for the vulgar is over-taken with
the appearance and event of a thing: and for the most part of
people, they are but the vulgar: the others that are but few,
take place where the vulgar have no subsistence. A Prince
there is in these days, whom I shall not do well to name, that

preaches nothing else but peace and faith; but had he kept the one and the other, several times had they taken from him his state and reputation.

In the sixteenth, seventeenth, and eighteenth Chap, our Author descends to particulars, perswading his Prince in his sixthenth to such a suppleness of disposition, as that upon occasion he can make use either of liberality or miserableness, as need shall require. But that of liberality is to last no longer than while he is in the way to some design: which if he well weigh, is not really a reward of virtue, how ere it seems; but a bait and lure to bring birds to the net. In the seventeenth Chap, he treats of clemency and cruelty, neither of which are to be exercis'd by him as acts of mercy or justice; but as they may serve to advantage his further purposes. And lest the Prince should incline too much to clemency, our Author allows rather the restraint by fear, than by love. The contrary to which all stories shew us. I will say this only, cruelty may cut of the power of some, but causes the hatred of all, and gives a will to most to take the first occasion offered for revenge. In the eighteenth Chap, our Author discourses how Princes ought to govern themselves in keeping their promises made: whereof he says they ought to make such small reckoning, as that rather they should know by their craft how to turn and wind men about, whereby to take advantage of all winds and fortunes. To this I would oppose that in the fifteenth Psal. v. 5. He that sweareth to his neighbor, and disappointeth him not, though it were to his own hindrance. It was a King that writ it, and me thinks the rule he gave, should well befit both King and Subject: and surely this perswades against all taking of advantages. A man may reduce all the causes of faith-breaking to three heads. One may be, because he that promised, had no intention to keep his word; and this is a wicked and malicious way of dealing. A second may be, because he that promised, repents of his promise made; and that is grounded on unconstancy, and lightness in that he would not be well resolved before he entered into covenant. The third may be, when it so falls out, that it lyes not in his power that made the promise to per-

form it. In which case a man ought to imitate the good debt-
or, who having not wherewithal to pay, hides not himself,
but presents his person to his creditor, willingly suffering
imprisonment. The first and second are very vicious and unworthy of a Prince: in the third, men might well be directed
by the examples of those two famous Romans, Regulus and
Posthumius. I shall close this with the answer of Charles the
fifth, when he was pressed to break his word with Luther for
his safe return from Wormes; Fides rerum promissarum etsi
toto mundo exulet, tamen apud imperatorem cam consistere
oportet. Though truth be banisht out of the whole world, yet
should it always find harbour in an Emperors breast.
Gulielmus Xenocarus in vit. Car. Quinti.

That Princes Should Take a Care, Not to Incur Contempt or Hatred

But because among the qualities, whereof formerly mention is made, I have spoken of those of most importance, I
will treat of the others more briefly under these qualities that
a Prince is to beware, as in part is above-said, and that he fly
those things which cause him to be odious or vile: and when
ever he shall avoid this, he shall fully have plaid his part,
and in the other disgraces he shall find no danger at all.
There is nothing makes him so odious, as I said, as his extor-
tion of his subjects goods, and abuse of their women, from
which he ought to forbear; and so long as he wrongs not his
whole people, neither in their goods, nor honors, they live
content, and he hath only to strive with the Ambition of some
few: which many ways and easily too, is restrain'd. To be
held various, light, effeminate, faint-hearted, unresolv'd,
these make him be contemnd and thought base, which a
Prince should shun like rocks, and take a care that in all his
actions there appear magnanimity, courage, gravity, and val-
or; and that in all the private affairs of his subjects, he orders
it so, that his word stand irrevocable: and maintain himself
in such repute, that no man may think either to deceive or
wind and turn him about: that Prince that gives such an
opinion of himself, is much esteemed, and against him who

is so well esteemed, hardly are any conspiracies made by his subjects, or by foreigners any invasion, when once notice is taken of his worth, and how much he is reverenced by his subjects: For a Prince ought to have two fears, the one from within, in regard of his subjects; the other from abroad, in regard of his mighty neighbors; from these he defends himself by good armies and good friends; and always he shall have good friends, if he have good armies; and all things shall always stand sure at home, when those abroad are firm, in case some conspiracy have not disturbed them; and however the foreign matters stand but ticklishly; yet if he have taken such courses at home, and liv'd as we have prescribed, he shall never be able (in case he forsake not himself) to resist all possibility, force and violence, as I said Nabis the Spartan did: but touching his subjects, even when his affairs abroad are settled, it is to be fear'd they may conspire privily; from which a Prince sufficiently secure himself by shunning to be hated or contemned, and keeping himself in his peoples good opinion, which it is necessary for him to compass, as formerly we treated at large. And one of the most powerful remedies a Prince can have against conspiracies, is, not to be hated nor despised by the universality; for always he that conspires, believes the Princes death is acceptable to the subject: but when he thinks it displeases them, he hath not the heart to venture on such a matter; for the difficulties that are on the conspirators side, are infinite. By experience it is plain, that many times plots have been laid, but few of them have succeeded luckily; for he that conspires, cannot be alone, nor can he take the company of any, but of those, who he believes are malcontents; and so soon as thou hast discover'd thy self to a malcontent, thou givest him means to work his own content: for by revealing thy treason, he may well hope for all manner of favour: so that seeing his gain certain of one side; and on the other, finding only doubt and danger, either he had need be a rare friend, or that he be an exceeding obstinate enemy to the Prince, if he keeps his word with the. And to reduce this matter into short terms: I say, there is nothing but jealousy, fear, and suspect of punishment on the conspirators part to affright him; but on the Princes part, there is the majesty of the principality, the laws, the defences of his friends and the State, which do so guard him, that to all these things the peoples good wills being added, it is impossible any one should be so head-strong as to conspire; for ordinarily where a traitor is to fear before the execution of his mischief, in this case he is also to fear afterwards, having the people for his enemy when the fact is committed, and therefore for this cause, not being able to hope for any refuge. Touching this matter, many examples might be brought; but I will content my self to name one which fell out in the memory of our Fathers. Annibal Bentivolii, grand Father of this Annibal who now lives, that was Prince in Bolonia, being slain by the Canneschi that conspir'd against him, none of his race being left, but this John, who was then in swaddling clouts; presently the people rose upon this murder, and slew all the Canneschi which proceeded from the popular affection, which the family of the Bentivolii held then in Bolonia: which was so great, that being there remain'd not any, now Anniball was dead, that was able to manage the State; and having notice that in Florence there was one borne of the Bentivolii, who till then was taken for a Smiths son: the citizens of Bolonia went to Florence for him, and gave the government of their City to him, which was rul'd by him, until John was of fit years to govern. I conclude then, that a Prince ought to make small account of treasons, whiles he hath the people to friend: but if they be his enemies and hate him, he may well fear every thing, and every one. And well ordered States, and discreet Princes have taken care withall diligence, not to cause their great men to fall into desperation, and to content the people, and so to maintain them: for this is one of the most important business belonging to a Prince. Among the Kingdoms that are well ordered and governed in our days, is that of France, and therein are found exceeding many good orders, whereupon the Kings liberty and security depends: of which the chief is the Parliament, and the authority thereof: for he that founded that Kingdom, knowing the great mens ambition and insolence; and judging it necessary there should be a bridle to curb them; and on the other side knowing the hatred of the Commonalty against the great ones, grounded upon fear, intending to secure them, would not lay this care wholly upon the King, but take this trouble from him, which he might have with the great men, in case he favoured the Commonalty; or with the Commonalty, in case he favoured the great men; and thereupon set up a third judge, which was that, to the end it should keep under the great ones, and favour the meaner sort, without any imputation to the King. It was not possible to take a better, nor wiser course then this; nor a surer way to secure the King, and the Kingdom. From whence we may draw another conclusion worthy of note, that Princes ought to cause others to take upon them the matters of blame and imputation; and upon themselves to take only those of grace and favour. Here again I conclude, that a Prince ought to make good esteem of his Nobility; but not thereby to incur the Commons hatred: It would seemed perhaps to many, considering the life and death of many Romane Emperours, that they were examples contrary to my opinion, finding that some have liv'd worthily, and showed many rare virtues of the mind, and yet have lost the Empire, and been put to death by their own subjects, conspiring against them. Intending then to answer these objections, I shall discourse upon the qualities of some Emperours, declaring the occasions of their ruin, not disagreeing from that which I have alleged; and part thereof I will bestow on the consideration of these things, which are worthy to be noted by him that reads the actions of those times: and it shall suffice me to take all those Emperours that succeeded in the Empire from Marcus the Philosopher to Maximinus, who were Mercus and Commodus his son, Pertinax, Julian, Severus, Antonius, Caracalla his son, Macrinus, Heliogabalus, Alexander, and Maximin. And first it is to be noted, that where in the other Principalities, they are to contend only with the ambition of the Nobles, and the insolence of the people; the Romane Emperours had a third difficulty, having to support the cruelty and covetousnesse of the soldiers, which was so hard a thing, that it caused the ruin of many, being hard to satisfy the soldiers, and the people; for the people love their quiet, and therefore affect modest Princes; and the soldiers love a Prince of a warlike courage, that is insolent, cruel, and plucking from every one: which things they would have them exercise upon the people, whereby they might be able to double their stipends, and satisfied their avarice and cruelty: whence it proceeds, that those Emperours who either by Nature or by Art, had not such a reputation, as therewith they could curb the one and the other, were always ruined: and the most of them, specially those who as new men came to the principality, finding the difficulty of those two different humours, applied themselves to content the soldiers, making small account of wronging the people, which was a course then necessary; for the Princes not being able to escape the hatred of every one, ought first endeavour that they incurre not the hatred of any whole universality; and when they cannot attain thereunto, they are to provide with all industry, to avoid the hatred of those universalities that are the most mighty. And therefore those Emperors, who because they were but newly call'd to the Empire, had need of extraordinary favours, more willingly stuck to the soldiers, than to the people; which nevertheless turned to their advantage, or otherwise, according as that Prince knew how to maintain his repute with them. From these causes aforesaid proceeded it, that Marcus Pertinax, and Alexander, though all living modestly, being lovers of justice, and enemies of cruelty, courteous and bountiful, had all from Marcus on ward, miserable ends; Marcus only liv'd and dy'd exceedingly honoured: for he came to the Empire by inheritance, and was not to acknowledge it either from the soldiers, nor from the people: afterwards being accompanied with many virtues, which made him venerable, he held always whilst he liv'd the one and the other order within their limits, and was never either hated, or contemned. But Pertinax was created Emperour against the soldiers wills, who being accustomed to live licentiously under Commodus, could not endure that honest course that Pertinax sought to reduce them to: Whereupon having gotten himself hatred, and to this hatred added contempt, in that he was old, was ruined in the very beginning of his government. Whence it ought to be observed, that hatred is gained as well by good deeds as bad; and therefore as I formerly said, when a Prince would maintain the State, he is often forced not to be good: for when that generality, whether it be the people, or soldiers, or Nobility, whereof thou thinkst thou standst in need to maintain the, is corrupted, it behoves the to follow their humour, and content them, and then all good deeds are thy adversaries. But let us come to Alexander who was of that goodness, that among the praises given him, had this for one, that in fourteen years wherein he held the Empire, he never put any man to death, but by course of justice; nevertheless being held effeminate, and a man that suffered himself to be ruled by his mother, and thereupon fallen into contempt, the army conspird against him. Now on the contrary discoursing upon the qualities of Commodus, Severus, Antonius, Caracalla, and Maximinus, you shall find them exceeding cruel, and ravenous, who to satisfy their soldiers, forbear no kind of injury that could be done upon the people; and all of them, except Severus, came to evil ends: for in Severus, there was such extraordinary valor, that while he held the soldiers his freinds, however the people were much burdened by him, he might always reigne happily: for his valor rendered him so admirable in the soldiers and peoples sights; that these in a manner stood amazed and astonished, and those others reverencing and honoring him. And because the actions of this man were exceeding great, being in a new Prince, I will briefly shew how well he knew to act the Foxes and the Lions parts; the conditions of which two, I say, as before, are very necessary for a Prince to imitate. Severus having had experience of Julian the Emperours sloth, persuaded his army (whereof he was commander in Sclavonia) that they should doe well to goe to Rome to revenge Pertinax his death, who was put to death by the Imperiall guard; and under this pretence, not making any shew that he aspird unto the Empire, set his army in march directly towards Rome, and was sooner come into It-

aly, than it was known he had mov'd from his station. Being
ariv'd at Rome, he was by the Senate chosen Emperour for
fear, and Julian slain. After this beginning, two difficulties
yet remained to Severus, before he could make himself Lord
of the whole State; the one in Asia, where Niger the General
of those armies had gotten the title of Emperour, the other in
the West with Albinus, who also aspird to the Empire: and
because he thought there might be some danger to discover
himself enemy to them both, he purposed to set upon Niger,
and cozen Albinus, to whom he writ, that being elected Emperour by the Senate, he would willingly communicate it with
him; and thereupon sent him the title of Cæsar, and by resolution of the Senate, took him to him for his Colleague; which
things were taken by Albinus in true meaning. But afterwards when Severus had overcome and slain Niger, and pac-
ified the Affairs and in the East, being returned to Rome, he
complained in the Senate of Albinus, how little weighing the
benefits received from him, he had sought to slay him by
treason, and therefore was he forc'd to goe punish his in-
gratitude: afterwards he went into France, where he bereft
him both of his State and life, whoever then shall in particular examine his actions, shall finde he was a very cruel Lion,
and as crafty a Fox: and shall see that he was always feared
and reverenc'd by every one, and by the armies not hated;
and shall nothing marvel that he being a new man, was able
to hold together such a great Empire: for his extraordinary
reputation defended him always from that hatred, which the
people for his extortions might have conceiv'd against him.
But Antonius his son, was also an exceeding brave man, and
endued with most excellent qualities, which causd him to be
admired by the people, and acceptable to the soldiers, because he was a warlike man, enduring all kind of travel and
pains, despising all delicate food, and all kind of effeminacy,
which gained him the love of all the armies: nevertheless his
fiercenesse and cruelty were such, and so hideous, having
upon many particular occasions put to death a great part of
the people of Rome, and all those of Alexandria, that he grew
odious to the world, and began to be feared by those also

that were near about him; so that he was slain by a Centurion in the very midst of his army. Where it is to be noted, that these kinde of deaths, which follow upon the deliberation of a resolv'd and obstinate mind, cannot by a Prince be avoided: for every one that fears not to dye, is able to doe it; but a Prince ought to be lesse afraid of it because it very seldom falls out. Only should he beware not to doe any extreme injury to any of those of whom he serves himself, or that he hath near about him in any employment of his Principality, as Antonius did: who had reproachfully slain a brother of that Centurion; also threatened him every day, and nevertheless entertained him still as one of the guards of his body, which was a rash course taken, and the way to destruction, as befell him. But let us come to Commodus for whom it was very easy to hold the Empire, by reason it descended upon him by inheritance, being Marcus his son, and it had been enough for him to follow his fathers footsteps, and then had he contented both the people and the soldiers: but being of a cruel and savage disposition, whereby to exercise his actions upon the people, he gave himself to entertain armies, and those in all licentiousnesse. On the other part not maintaining his dignity, but often descending upon the stages to combat with fencers, and doing such other like base things, little worthy of the Imperiall majesty, he became contemptible in the soldiers sight; and being hated of one part, and despised of the other, he was conspird against, and slain. It remains now, that we declare Maximinus his conditions, who was a very warlike man; and the armies loathing Alexanders effeminacy, whereof I spake before, when they had slain him, chose this man Emperour, who not long continued so, because two things there were that brought him into hatred and contempt; the one because he was very base, having kept cattell in Thrace, which was well known to every one, and made them to scorn him; the other, because in the beginning of his Principality having delayed to go to Rome, and enter into possession of the Imperiall throne, he had gained the infamy of being thought exceeding cruel, having by his Prefects in Rome, and in every place of the Empire, exercised many cruelties, insomuch that the whole world being provok'd against him to contempt for the basenesse of his blood; on the other side upon the hatred conceiv'd against him for fear of his cruelty; first Affrica, afterwards the Senate, with all the people of Rome and all Italy, conspired against him, with whom his own army took part; which encamping before Aquileya, and finding some difficulty to take the town, being weary of his cruelties, and because they saw he had so many enemies, fearing him the lesse, slew him. I purpose not to say any thing either of Heliogabalus, Macrinus, or Julian, who because they were thoroughly base, were suddenly extinguished: but I will come to the conclusion of this discourse; and I say, that the Princes of our times have less of this difficulty to satisfy the Soldiers extraordinarily in their government; for notwithstanding that there be some considerations to be had of them, yet presently are those armies dissolved, because none of these Princes do use to maintain any armies together, which are annex'd and inveterated with the governments of the provinces, as were the armies of the Romane Empire. And therefore if then it was necessary rather to content the soldiers than the people, it was because the soldiers were more powerful than the people: now is it more necessary for all Princes, (except the Turk and the Souldan) to satisfy their people than their soldiers, because the people are more mighty than they; wherein I except the Turk, he always maintaining about his person 12000 foot, and 15000 horse, upon which depends the safety and strength of his Kingdom; and it is necessary that laying aside all other regard of his people, he maintain these his friends. The Souldans Kingdom is like hereunto, which being wholly in the soldiers power, he must also without respect of his people keep them his friends. And you are to consider, that this State of the Souldans differs much from all the other Principalities: For it is very like the Papacy, which cannot be termd an hereditary Principality: nor a new Principality: for the sons of the deceased Prince are not heirs and Lords thereof, but he that is chosen receives that dignity from those who have the authority in them. And this order being of antiquity, cannot be termed a new Principality, because therein are none of those difficulties that are in new ones: for though the Prince be new, yet are the orders of that state ancient, and ordained to receive him, as if he were their hereditary Prince. But let us return to our matter; whosoever shall consider our discourse before, shall perceive that either hatred, or contempt have caused the ruin of the afore-named Emperors; and shall know also, from it came that part of them proceeding one way, and part a contrary; yet in any of them the one had a happy success, and the others unhappy: for it was of no a vale, but rather hurtful for Pertinax and Alexander, because they were new Princes, to desire to imitate Marcus, who by inheritance came to the Principality: and in like manner it was a wrong to Caracalla, Commodus, and Maximus, to imitate Severus, because none of them were endued with so great valor as to follow his steps therein. Wherefore a new Prince in his Principality cannot well imitate Marcus his actions; nor yet is it necessary to follow those of Severus: but he ought make choice of those parts in Severus which are necessary for the founding of a State; and to take from Marcus those that are fit and glorious to preserve a State which is already established and settled.

Whether the Citadels and Many Other Things Which Princes Often Make Use Of, Are Profitable or Dammageable

Some Princes, whereby they might safely keep their State, have disarmed their subjects; some others have held the towns under their dominion, divided into factions; others have maintain'd enmities against themselves; others have appli'd themselves to gain them, where they have suspected at their entrance into the government; others have built Fortresses; and others again have ruined and demolished them: and however that upon all these things, a man cannot well pass a determinate sentence, unless one comes to the particulars of these States, where some such like determinations were to be taken; yet I shall speak of them in so large a manner, as the matter of it self will bear. It was never then that a new Prince would disarm his own subjects; but rather when he hath found them disarmed, he hath always arm'd them. For being belov'd, those armies become thine; those become faithful, which thou hadst in suspicion; and those which were faithful, are maintained so; and thy subjects are made thy partisans; and because all thy subjects cannot be put in armies, when thou bestowest favors on those thou armiest, with the others thou canst deal more for thy safety; and that difference of proceeding which they know among them, obliges them to the; those others excuse the, judging it necessary that they have deserved more, who have undergone more danger, and so have greater obligation: but when thou disarmst them, thou beginst to offend them, that thou distrustest them, either for cowardice, or small faith; and the one or the other of those two opinions provokes their hatred against the; and because thou canst not stand disarmed, thou must then turn thy self to mercenary Soldiery, whereof we have formerly spoken what it is, and when it is good; it can never be so much as to defend the from powerful enemies, and suspected subjects; therefore as I have said, a new Prince in a new Principality hath always ordaind them armies. Of examples to this purpose, Histories are full. But when a Prince gains a new State, which as a member he adds to his ancient dominions, then it is necessary to disarm that State, unless it be those whom thou hast discovered to have assisted the in the conquest thereof; and these also in time and upon occasions, it is necessary to render delicate and effeminate, and so order them, that all the arms of thy State be in the hands of thy own Soldiers, who live in thy ancient State near unto the. Our ancestors and they that were accounted Sages, were wont to say that it was necessary to hold Pistoya in factions, and Pisa with Fortresses; and for this cause maintained some towns subject to them in differences, whereby to hold it more easily. This, at what time Italy was ballanc'd in a certain manner, might be well done; but mee thinks it cannot now a days be well given for a precept; for I do not believe, that divisions made can do any good; rather it must needs be, that when the enemy approaches them, Cities divided are presently lost; for always the weaker part will cleave to the foreign power, and the other not be able to subsist. The Venetians (as I think) mov'd by the aforesaid reasons, maintained the factions of the Guelfes and Gibellins, in their towns; and however they never suffered them to spill one anothers blood, yet they nourish'd these differences among them, to the end that the citizens employed in these quarrels, should not plot any thing against them: which as it proved, never serv'd them to any great purpose: for being defeated at Vayla, presently one of those two factions took courage and seized upon their whole State. Therefore such like ways argue the Princes weakness; for in a strong principality they never will suffer such divisions; for they shew them some kind of profit in time of peace, being they are able by means thereof more easily to mannage their subjects: but war coming, such like orders discover their fallacy. Without doubt, Princes become great, when they overcome the difficulties and oppositions that are made against them; and therefore Fortune especially when she hath to make any new Prince great, who hath more need to gain reputation than an hereditary Prince, causes enemies to rise against him, and him to undertake against them: to the end he may have occasion to master them, and know that ladder, which his enemies have set him upon, whereby to rise yet higher. And therefore many think, that a wise Prince when he hath the occasion, ought cunningly to nourish some enmity, that by the suppressing thereof, his greatness may grow thereupon. Princes, especially those that are new, have found more faith and profit in those men, who in the beginning of their State, have been held suspected, than in those who at their entrance have been their confidantes. Pandulphus Petrucci, Prince of Siena, governed his State, more with them that had been suspected by him, than with the others. But of this matter we cannot speak at large, because it varies according to the subject; I will only say this, that those men, who in the beginning of a Principality were once enemies, if they be of quality so that to maintain themselves they have need of support, the Prince might always with the greatest facility gain for his; and they are the rather forced to serve him faithfully, insomuch as they know it is more necessary for them by their deeds to cancel that sinister opinion, which was once held of them; and so the Prince ever draws from these more advantage, than from those, who serving him too supinely, neglect his affairs. And seeing the matter requires it, I will not omit to put a Prince in mind, who hath anew made himself master of a State, by means of the inward helps he had from thence that he consider well the cause that mov'd them that favor'd him to favor him, if it be not a natural affection towards him; for if it be only because they were not content with their former government, with much pains and difficulties shall he be able to keep them long his friends, because it will be impossible for him to content them. By these examples then which are drawn out of ancient and modern Affairs, searching into the cause hereof, we shall find it much more easy to gain those men for friends, who formerly were contented with the State, and therefore were his enemies: than those, who because they were not contented therewith, became his fiends, and favor'd him in getting the mastery of it. It hath been the custom of Princes, whereby to hold their States more securely, to build Citadels, which might be bridles and curbs to those that should purpose any thing against them, and so to have a secure retreat from the first violences. I commend this course, because it hath been used of old; notwithstanding Nicholas Vitelli in our days hath been known to demolish two Citadels in the town of Castello, the better to keep the State; Guidubaldo Duke of Urbin being to return into his State, out of which he was driven by Cæsar Borgia, raz'd all the Fortresses of that Country, and thought he should hardlyer lose that State again without them. The Bentivolii returning into Bolonia, used the like courses. Citadels then are profitable, or not, according to the times; and if they advantage the in one part, they do the harm in another; and this part may be argued thus. That Prince who stands more in fear of his own people than of strangers, ought to build Fortresses: but he that is more afraid of strangers than of his people, should let them alone. Against the house of Sforza, the Castle of Milan, which Francis Sforza built, hath and will make more war, than any other disorder in that State: and therefore the best Citadel that may be, is not to incurred the peoples hatred; for however thou holdest a Fortress, and the people hate the, thou canst hardly escape them; for people, when once they have taken armies, never want the help of strangers at their need to take ther parts. In our days we never saw that they ever profited any Prince, unless it were the Countess of Furli, when Count Hieronymo of Furli her husband was slain; for by means thereof she escap'd the peoples rage, and attended aid from Milan, and so recover'd her State: and then such were the times that the stranger could not assist the people: but afterwards they serv'd her to little purpose, when Cæsar Borgia assaild her, and that the people which was her enemy, sided with the stranger. Therefore both then, and at first, it would have been more for her safety, not to have been odious to the people, than to have held the Fortresses. These things being well weigh'd then, I will commend those that shall build up Fortresses, and him also that shall not; and I will blame him, howsoever he be, that relying upon those, shall make small account of being hated by his people.

How a Prince Ought to Behave Himself to Gain Reputation

There is nothing gains a Prince such repute as great exploits, and rare trials of himself in Heroick actions. We have now in our days Ferdinand King of Arragon the present King of Spain: he in a manner may be termed a new Prince; for from a very weak King, he is now become for fame and glory, the first King of Christendome, and if you shall well consider his actions, you shall find them all illustrious, and every one of them extraordinary. He in the beginning of his reign assailed Granada, and that exploit was the ground of his State. At first he made that war in security, and without suspicion he should be any ways hindered, and therein held the Barons of Castiglias minds busied, who thinking upon that war, never minded any innovation; in this while he gained credit and authority with them, they not being aware of it; was able to maintain with the Church and the peoples money all his soldiers, and to lay a foundation for his military ordinances with that long war, which afterwards gained him exceeding much honor. Besides this, to the end he might be able here among to undertake greater matters, serving himself always of the colour of religion, he gave himself to a kind of religious cruelty, chasing and despoiling those Jews out of the Kingdom; nor can this example be more admirable and rare: under the same cloak he invaded Affrick and went through with his exploit in Italy: and last of all hath he assailed France, and so always proceeded on forwards contriving of great matters, which always have held his subjects minds in peace and admiration, and busied in attending the event, what it should be: and these his actions have thus grown, one upon another, that they have never given leisure to men so to rest, as they might ever plot any thing against them. Moreover it much avails a Prince to give extraordinary proofs of himself touching the government within, such as those we have heard of Bernard of Milan, whensoever occasion is given by any one, that may effectuate some great thing either of good or evil, in the civil government; and to find out some way either to reward or punish it, whereof in the world much notice may be taken. And above all things a Prince ought to endeavor in all his actions to spread abroad a fame of his magnificence and worthiness. A Prince also is well esteemed, when he is a true friend, or a true enemy; when without any regard he discovers himself in favor of one against another; which course shall be always more profit, than to stand neuter: for if two mighty ones that are thy neighbors, come to fall out, or are of such quality, that one of them vanquishing, thou art like to be in fear of the vanquisher, or not; in either of these two cases, it will ever prove more for thy profit, to discover thy self, and make a good war of it: for in the first case, if thou discoverest not thy self, thou shalt always be a prey to him that overcomes, to the contentment and satisfaction of the vanquished; neither shalt thou have reason on thy side, nor any thing else to defend or receive the. For he that overcomes, will not have any suspected

friends that give him no assistance in his necessity: and he
that loses, receives the not, because thou wouldest not with
thy armies in hand run the hazard of his fortune. Antiochus
passed into Greece, thereunto induc'd by the Etolians, to
chace the Romans thence: and sent his Ambassadors to the
Achayans, who were the Romans friends, to persuade them
to stand neuters; on the other side the Romans moved them
to joyne armies with theirs: this matter came to be deliber-
ated on in the council of the Achayans, where Antiochus his
Ambassador encouraged them to stand neuters, whereunto
the Romans Ambassador answered; Touching the course,
that is commended to you, as best and profitablest for your
State, to wit, not to intermeddle in the war between us, nothing can be more against you: because, not taking either part,
you shall remain without thanks, and without reputation a
prey to the conqueror. And it will always come to pass that
he who is not thy friend, will requite thy neutrality; and he
that is thy friend, will urge the to discover thy self by taking
arms for him: and evil advised Princes; to avoid the present
dangers, follow often times that way of neutrality, and most
commonly go to ruin: but when a Prince discovers himself
strongly in favor of a party; if he to whom thou cleavest,
overcomes; however that he be puissant, and thou remainest
at his disposing, he is oblig'd to the, and there is a contract
of friendship made; and men are never so openly dishonest,
as with such a notorious example of dishonesty to oppress
the. Besides victories are never so prosperous, that the conqueror is like neglect all respects, and especially of justice.
But if he to whom thou stickst, loses, thou art received by
him; and, while he is able, he aides the, and so thou becomest partner of a fortune that may arise again; the second
case, when they that enter into the lists together, are of such
quality, that thou needest not fear him that vanquisheth,
so much the more is it discretion in the to stick to him; for
thou goest to ruin one with his assistance, who ought to do
the best he could to save him, if he were well advised; and he
overcoming, is left at thy discretion; and it is unpossible but
with thy aid he must overcome. And here it is to be noted,

that a Prince should be well aware never to joyn with any one more powerful than himself, to offend another, unless upon necessity, as formerly is said. For when he overcomes, thou art left at his discretion, and Princes ought avoid as much as they are able, to stand at anothers discretion. The Venetians took part with France against the Duke of Milan, and yet could have avoided that partaking, from which proceeded their ruin. But when it cannot be avoided, as it befell the Florentines when the Pope and the King of Spain went both with their armies to Lombardy, there the Prince ought to side with them for the reasons aforesaid. Nor let any State think they are able to make such sure parties, but rather that they are all doubtful; for in the order of things we find it always, that whensoever a man seeks to avoid one inconvenient, he incurs another. But the principal point of judgement, is in discerning between the qualities of inconveniences, and not taking the bad for the good. Moreover a Prince ought to shew himself a lover of virtue, and that he honors those that excel in every Art. Afterwards ought he encourage his Citizens, whereby they may be enabled quickly to exercise their faculties as well in merchandise, and husbandry, as in any other kind of traffic, to the end that no man forbear to adorn and cultivate his possessions for fear that he be despoiled of them; or any other to open the commerce upon the danger of heavy impositions: but rather to provide rewards for those that shall set these matters afoot, or for any one else that shall any way amplify his City or State. Besides he ought in the fit times of the year entertain the people with Feasts and Maskes; and because every City is divided into Companies, and arts, and Tribes, he ought to take special notice of those bodies, and some times afford them a meeting, and give them some proof of his humanity, and magnificence; yet with all holding firm the majesty of his State; for this must never fail in any case.

Touching Princes Secretaries

It is no small importance to a Prince, the choice he makes, of servants being ordinarily good or bad, as his wisdom is.

And the first conjecture one gives of a great man, and of his understanding, is, upon the sight of his followers and servants he hath about him, when they prove able and faithful, and then may he always be reputed wise because he hath known how to discern those that are able, and to keep them true to him. But when they are otherwise, there can be no good conjecture made of him; for the first error he commits, is in this choice. There was no man that had any knowledge of Antonio of Vanafro, the servant of Pandulfus Petrucci Prince of Sicily, who did not esteem Pandulfus for a very discreet man, having him for his servant. And because there are three kinds of understandings; the one that is advised by it self; the other that understands when it is informed by another; the third that neither is advised by it self nor by the demonstration of another; the first is best, the second is good, and the last quite unprofitable. Therefore it was of necessity, that if Pandulfus attained not the first degree, yet he got to the second; for whenever any one hath the judgement to discern between the good and the evil, that he does and says, however that he hath not his distinction from himself, yet still comes he to take notice of the good or evil actions of that servant; and those he cherishes, and these he suppresses; insomuch that the servant finding no means to deceive his master, keeps himself upright and honest. But how a Prince may thoroughly understand his servant, here is the way that never fails. When thou seest the servant study more for his own advantage than thine, and that in all his actions, he searches most after his own profit; this man thus qualified, shall never prove good servant, nor canst thou ever relie upon him: for he that holds the Sterne of the State in hand, ought never call home his cares to his own particular, but give himself wholly over to his Princes service, nor ever put him in mind of any thing not appertaining to him. And on the other side the Prince to keep him good to him, ought to take a care for his servant, honoring him, enriching, and obliging him to him, giving him part both of dignities and offices, to the end that the many honors and much wealth bestowed on him, may restrain his desires from other honors, and other wealth, and that those many charges cause him to fear changes that may fall, knowing he is not able to stand without his master. And when both the Princes and the servants are thus disposed, they may rely the one upon the other: when otherwise, the end will ever prove hurtful for the one as well as for the other.

That Flatterers Are to Be Avoided

I will not omit one principle of great importance, being an error from which Princes with much difficulty defend themselves, unless they be very discreet, and make a very good choice; and this is concerning flatterers; whereof all writings are full: and that because men please themselves so much in their own things, and therein cozen themselves, that very hardly can they escape this pestilence; and desiring to escape it, there is danger of falling into contempt; for there is no other way to be secure from flattery, but to let men know, that they displease the not in telling the truth: but when every one hath this leave, thou losest thy reverence. Therefore ought a wise Prince take a third course, making choice of some understanding men in his State, and give only to them a free liberty of speaking to him the truth; and touching those things only which he inquires of, and nothing else; but he ought to be inquisitive of every thing, and hear their opinions, and then afterwards advise himself after his own manner; and in these deliberations, and with every one of them so carry himself, that they all know, that the more freely they shall speak, the better they shall be liked of: and besides those, not give eare to any one; and thus pursue the thing resolved on, and thence continue obstinate in the resolution taken. He who does otherwise, either falls upon flatterers, or often changes upon the varying of opinions, from whence proceeds it that men conceive but slightly of him. To this purpose I will allege you a modern example. Peter Lucas a servant of Maximilians the present Emperor, speaking of his Majesty, said that he never advised with any body, nor never did any thing after his own way: which was because he took a contrary course to what we have now said: for the

Emperor is a close man, who communicates his secrets to none, nor takes counsel of any one; but as they come to be put in practise, they begin to be discovered and known, and so contradicted by those that are near about him; and he as being an easy man, is quickly wrought from them. Whence it comes that what he does to day, he undoes on the morrow; and that he never understands himself what he would, nor what he purposes, and that there is no grounding upon any of his resolutions. A Prince therefore ought always to take counsel, but at his own pleasure, and not at other mens; or rather should take away any mans courage to advise him of any thing, but what he asks: but he ought well to ask at large, and then touching the things inquired of, be a patient hearer of the truth; and perceiving that for some respect the truth were concealed from him, be displeased thereat. And because some men have thought that a Prince that gains the opinion to be wise, may be held so, not by his own natural endowments, but by the good counsels he hath about him; without question they are deceived; for this is a general rule and never fails, that a Prince who of himself is not wise, can never be well advised, unless he should light upon one alone, wholly to direct and govern him, who himself were a very wise man. In this case it is possible he may be well governed: but this would last but little: for that governor in a short time would deprive him of his State; but a Prince not having any parts of nature, being advised of more then one, shall never be able to unite these counsels: of himself shall he never know how to unite them; and each one of the Counsellers, probably will follow that which is most properly his own; and he shall never find the means to amend or discern these things; nor can they fall out otherwise, because men always prove mischievous, unless upon some necessity they be forc'd to become good: we conclude therefore, that counsels from whencesoever they proceed, must needs take their beginning from the Princes wisdom, and not the wisdom of the Prince from good counsels.

In this Chapter our Authour prescribes some rules how to avoid flattery, and not to fall into contempt. The extent of

these two extremes is so large on both sides, that there is left
but a very narrow path for the right temper to walk between
them both: and happy were that Prince, who could light on
so good a Pilote as to bring him to Port between those rocks
and those quicksands. Where Majesty becomes familiar, unless endued with a super-eminent virtue, it loses all awful
regards: as the light of the Sunne, because so ordinary, because so common, we should little value, were it not that all
Creatures feel themselves quickned by the rayes thereof. On
the other side, Omnis insipiens arrogantiâ et plausibus ca-
pitur, Every fool is taken with his own pride and others flat-
teryes: and this fool keeps company so much with all great
wise men, that hardly with a candle and lantern can they
be discern betwixt. The greatest men are more subject to
gross and palpable flatteries; and especially the greatest of
men, who are Kings and Princes: for many seek the Rulers
favour. Prov. 28. 26. For there are divers means whereby private men are instructed; Princes have not that good hap: but
they whose instruction is of most importance, so soone as
they have taken the government upon them, no longer suffer any reproovers: for but few have access unto them, and
they who familiarly converse with them, doe and say all for
favour. Isocrat, to Nicocles, All are afraid to give him occasion of displeasure, though by telling him truth. To this purpose therefore says one; a Prince excels in learning to ride
the great horse, rather than in any other exercise, because
his horse being no flatterer, will shew him he makes no difference between him and another man, and unless he keep
his seat well, will lay him on the ground. This is plain dealing. Men are more subtile, more double-heartd, they have a
heart and a heart neither is their tongue their hearts true
interpreter. Counsell in the heart of man is like deep waters;
but a man of understanding will draw it out. Prov. 20. 5.
This understanding is most requisite in a Prince, inasmuch
as the whole Globe is in his hand, and the inferior Orbes are
swayed by the motion of the highest. And therefore surely it
is the honour of a King to search out such a secret: Prov.
25. 2. His counselors are his eyes and eares; as they ought

to be dear to him, so they ought to be true to him, and make him the true report of things without disguise. If they prove false eyes, let him pluck them out; he may as they use glass eyes, take them forth without paine, and see never a whit the worse for it. The wisdom of a Princes Counsellours is a great argument of the Princes wisdom. And being the choice of them imports the Princes credit and safety, our Authour will make him amends for his other errour by his good advice in his 22 Chap. whether I refer him.

Wherefore the Princes of Italy Have Lost Their States

When these things above said are well observ'd, they make a new Prince seem as if he had been of old, and presently render him more secure and firm in the State, than if he had already grown ancient therein: for a new Prince is much more observed in his action, than a Prince by inheritance; and when they are known to be vertuous, men are much more gained and oblig'd to them thereby, than by the antiquity of their blood: for men are much more taken by things present, than by things past, and when in the present they find good, they content themselves therein, and seek no further; or rather they undertake the defence of him to their utmost, when the Prince is not wanting in other matters to himself; and so shall he gain double glory to have given a beginning to a new Principality, adorned, and strengthened it with good laws, good arms, good friends, and good examples; as he shall have double shame, that is born a Prince, and by reason of his small discretion hath lost it. And if we shall consider those Lords, that in Italy have lost their States in our days, as the King of Naples, the Duke of Milan, and others; first we shall find in them a common defect, touching their armies, for the reasons which have been above discoursed at length. Afterwards we shall see some of them, that either shall have had the people for their enemies; or be it they had the people to friend, could never know how to assure themselves of the great ones: for without such defects as these, States are not lost, which have so many nerves, that they are able to maintain an army in the field. Philip of Macedon, not the father of Alexander the Great, but he that was vanquished by Titus Quintius, had not much State in regard of the greatness of the Romanes and of Greece that assail'd him; nevertheless in that he was a warlike man and knew how to entertained the people, and assure himself of the Nobles, for many years he made the war good against them: and though at last some town perhaps were taken from him, yet the Kingdom remained in his hands still. Wherefore these our Princes who for many years had continued in their Principalities, for having afterwards lost them, let them not blame Fortune, but their own sloth; because they never having thought during the time of quiet, that they could suffer a change (which is the common fault of men, while faire weather lasts, not to provide for the tempest) when afterwards mischiefs came upon them, thought rather upon flying from them, than upon their defence, and hop'd that the people, weary of the vanquishers insolence, would recall them: which course when the others fail, is good: but very ill is it to leave the other remedies for that: for a man wou'd never go to fall, believing another would come to take him up: which may either not come to passe, or if it does, it is not for thy security, because that defence of his is vile, and depends not upon the; but those defences only are good, certain, and durable, which depend upon thy own self, and thy own virtues.

How Great Power Fortune Hath in Humane Affairs, and What Means There Is to Resist it

It is not unknown unto me, how that many have held opinion, and still hold it, that the Affairs of the world are so governed by fortune, and by God, that men by their wisdom cannot amend or alter them; or rather that there is no remedy for them: and hereupon they would think that it were of no avail to take much pains in any thing, but leave all to be governed by chance. This opinion hath gain'd the more credit in our days, by reason of the great alteration of things, which we have of late seen, and do every day see, beyond all humane conjecture: upon which, I sometimes thinking,

am in some part inclined to their opinion: nevertheless not
to extinguish quite our own free will, I think it may be true,
that Fortune is the mistress of one half of our actions; but
yet that she lets us have rule of the other half, or little less.
And I liken her to a precipitous torrent, which when it rages,
over-flows the planes, overthrows the trees, and buildings,
removes the earth from one side, and lays it on another, every one flies before it, every one yields to the fury thereof, as
unable to withstand it; and yet however it be thus, when the
times are calmer, men are able to make provision against
these excesses, with banks and fences so, that afterwards
when it swels again, it shall all passe smoothly along, within its channel, or else the violence thereof shall not prove
so licentious and hurtfull. In like manner befalls it us with
fortune, which there shewes her power where virtue is not
ordained to resist her, and thither turns she all her forces,
where she perceives that no provisions nor resistances are
made to uphold her. And if you shall consider Italy, which is
the seat of these changes, and that which hath given them
their motions, you shall see it to be a plain field, without any
trench or bank; which had it been fenc'd with convenient
virtue as was Germany, Spain or France; this inundation
would never have caused these great alterations it hath, or
else would it not have reach'd to us: and this shall suffice to
have said, touching the opposing of fortune in general. But
restraining my self more to particulars, I say that to day we
see a Prince prosper and flourish and to morrow utterly go to
ruin; not seeing that he hath altered any condition or quality; which I believe arises first from the causes which we have
long since run over, that is because that Prince that relies
wholly upon fortune, runes as her wheel turns. I believe also,
that he proves the fortunate man, whose manner of proceeding meets with the quality of the time; and so likewise he
unfortunate from whose course of proceeding the times differ: for we see that men, in the things that induce them to
the end, (which every one propounds to himself, as glory and
riches) proceed therein diversely; some with respects, others
more bold, and rashly; one with violence, and th'other with

cunning; the one with patience, th'other with its contrary; and every one of several ways may attain thereto; we see also two very respective and wary men, the one come to his purpose, and th'other not; and in like manner two equally prosper, taking divers course; the one being wary the other head-strong; which proceeds from nothing else, but from the quality of the times, which agree, or not, with their proceedings. From hence arises that which I said, that two working diversely, produce the same effect: and two equally working, the one attains his end, the other not. Hereupon depends the alteration of the good; for if to one that behaves himself with wariness and patience, times and Affairs turn so favourably, that the carriage of his business prove well, he prospers; but if the times and Affairs chance, he is ruined, because he changes not his manner of proceeding: nor is there any man so wise, that can frame himself hereunto; as well because he cannot go out of the way, from that whereunto Nature inclines him: as also, for that one having always prospered, walking such a way, cannot be persuaded to leave it; and therefore the respective and wary man, when it is fit time for him to use violence and force, knows not how to put it in practice, whereupon he is ruined: but if he could change his disposition with the times and the Affairs, he should not change his fortune. Pope Julius the second proceeded in all his actions with very great violence, and found the times and things so conformable to that his manner of proceeding that in all of them he had happy success. Consider the first exploit he did at Bolonia, even while John Bentivolio lived: the Venetians were not well contented therewith; the King of Spaine likewise with the French, had treated of that enterprise; and notwithstanding al this, he stirrd up by his own rage and fierceness, personally undertook that expedition: which action of his put in suspense and stopped Spain and the Venetians; those for fear, and the others for desire to recover the Kingdom of Naples; and on the other part drew after him the King of France; for that King seeing him already in motion, and desiring to hold him his friend, whereby to humble the Venetians, thought he could no way deny him his soldiers, without doing him an open injury. Julius then effected that with his violent and heady motion, which no other Pope with all humane wisdom could ever have done; for if he had expected to part from Rome with his conclusions settled, and all his Affairs ordered before hand, as any other Pope would have done, he had never brought it to passe: For the King of France would have devised a thousand excuses, and others would have put him in as many fears. I will let passe his other actions, for all of them were alike, and all of them prov'd lucky to him; and the brevity of his life never suffered him to feel the contrary: for had he litt upon such times afterwards, that it had been necessary for him to proceed with respects, there had been his utter ruin; for he would never have left those ways, to which he had been naturally inclined. I conclude then, fortune varying, and men continuing still obstinate to their own ways, prove happy, while these accord together: and as they disagree, prove unhappy: and I think it true, that it is better to be heady than wary; because Fortune is a mistresse; and it is necessary, to keep her in obedience to ruffle and force her: and we see, that she suffers her self rather to be masterd by those, than by others that proceed coldly. And therefore, as a mistress, she is a friend to young men, because they are lesse respective, more rough, and command her with more boldnesse.

I have considered the 25 Chapter, as representing me a full view of humane policy and cunning: yet me thinks it cannot satisfied a Christian in the causes of the good and bad success of things. The life of man is like a game at Tables; skill avails much I grant, but that's not all: play thy game well, but that will not win: the chance thou throwest must accord with thy play. Examine this; play never so surely, play never so probably, unless the chance thou castest, lead the forward to advantage, all hazards are losses, and thy sure play leaves the in the lurch. The sum of this is set down in Ecclesiastes chap. 9. v. 11. The race is not to the swift, nor the battle to the strong: neither yet bread to the wise, nor yet riches to men of understanding, nor yet favour to men of skill; but time and chance hapeneth to them all. Our cunning Author for all his exact rules he deliver in his books, could not fence against the despight of Fortune, as he complains in his Epistle to this book. Nor that great example of policy, Duke Valentine, whom our Author commends to Princes for his crafts-master, could so ruffle or force his mistress Fortune, that he could keep her in obedience. Man can contribute no more to his actions than virtue and wisdom: but the success depends upon a power above. Surely there is the finger of god; or as Prov. 16. v. 33. 'The lot is cast into the lap, but the whole disposing thereof is of the Lord.' It was not Josephs wisdom made all things thrive under his hand; but because the Lord was with him; and that which he did, the Lord made it to prosper, Gen. 39. Surely this is a blessing proceeding from the divine providence, which beyond humane capacity so cooperateth with the causes, as that their effects prove answerable, and sometimes (that we may know there is something above the ordinary causes) the success returns with such a supremacy of worth, that it far exceeds the virtue of the ordinary causes.

An Exhortation to Free Italy from the Barbarians

Having then weighed all things above discours'd, and devising with my self, whether at this present in Italy the time might serve to honor a new Prince, and whether there were matter that might minister occasion to a wise and valorous Prince, to introduce such a form, that might do honor to him, and good to the whole generality of the people in the country: me thinks so many things concurre in favor of a new Prince, that I know not whether there were ever any time more proper for this purpose. And if as I said, it was necessary, desiring to see Moses his virtue, that the children of Israel should be inthrald in Ægypt; and to have experience of the magnanimity of Cyrus his mind, that the Persians should be oppress'd by the Medes; and to set forth the excellency of Theseus, that the Athenians should be dispersed; so at this present now we are desirous to know the valor of an Italian spirit, it were necessary Italy should be reduc'd to the same terms it is now in, and were in more slavery than the Hebrews were; more subject than the Persians, more scattered than the Athenians; without head, without order, battered, pillaged, rent asunder, overrun, and had undergone all kind of destruction. And however even in these later days, we have had some kind of shew of hope in some one, whereby we might have conjectur'd, that he had been ordained for the deliverance hereof, yet it prov'd afterwards, that in the very height of all his actions he was curb'd by fortune, insomuch that this poor country remaining as it were without life, attends still for him that shall heal her wounds, give an end to all those pillagings and sackings of Lombardy, to those robberies and taxations of the Kingdom, and of Tuscany, and heal them of their soars, now this long time gangren'd. We see how she makes her prayers to God, that he send some one to redeem her from these Barbarous cruelties and insolencies. We see her also wholly ready and disposed to follow any colours, provided there be any one take them up. Nor do we see at this present, that she can look for other, than your Illustrious Family, to become Chieftain of this deliverance, which hath now by its own virtue and Fortune been so much exalted, and favored by God and the Church, whereof it now holds the Principality: and this shall not be very hard for you to do, if you shall call to mind the former actions, and lives of those that are above named. And though those men were very rare and admirable, yet were they men, and every one of them began upon less occasion than this; for neither was their enterprise more just than this, nor more easy; nor was God more their friend, than yours. Here is very great justice: for that war is just, that is necessary; and those armies are religious, when there is no hope left otherwhere, but in them. Here is an exceeding good disposition thereto: nor can there be, where there is a good disposition, a giant difficulty, provided that use be made of those orders, which I propounded for aim and direction to you. Besides this, here we see extraordinary things without example effected by God; the sea was opened, a cloud guided the way, devotion poured forth the waters, and it rain'd down Manna; all these things have concurred in your greatness, the rest is left for you to do. God will not do every thing himself, that he may not take from us our free will, and of that glory that belongs to us. Neither is it a marvel, if any of the afore named Italians have not been able to compass that, which we may hope your illustrious family shall: though in so many revolutions of Italy, and so many feats of war, it may seem that the whole military virtue therein be quite extinguished; for this arises from that the ancient orders thereof were not good; and there hath since been none that hath known how to invent new ones. Nothing can so much honor a man rising anew, as new laws and new ordinances devised by him: these things when they have a good foundation given them, and contain in them their due greatness, gain him reverence and admiration; and in Italy their wants not the matter wherein to introduce any form. Here is great virtue in the members, were it not wanting in the heads. Consider in the single fights that have been, and duels, how much the Italians have excel'd in their strength, activity and address; but when they come to armies, they appear not, and all proceeds from the weakness of the Chieftains; for they that understand the managing of these matters, are not obeyed; and every one presumes to understand; hitherto there having not been any one so highly raised either by fortune or virtue, as that others would submit unto him. From hence proceeds it, that in so long time, and in so many battles fought for these last past 20 years, when there hath been an army wholly Italian, it always hath had evil success; whereof the river Tarus first was witness, afterwards Alexandria, Capua, Genua, Vayla, Bolonia, Mestri. Your Illustrious family then being desirous to tread the footsteps of these Worthyes who redeem'd their countries, must above all things as the very foundation of the whole fabric, be furnished with soldiers of your own natives: because you cannot have more faithful, true, nor better soldiers; and though every one of them be good, all together they will become better when they shall find themselves entertained, commanded, and honored by their own Prince. Wherefore it is necessary to provide for those armies, whereby to be able with the Italian valor to make a defence against foreigners. And however

the Swiss infantry and Spanish be accounted terrible; yet is
there defect in both of them, by which a third order might not
only oppose them, but may be confident to vanquish them:
for the Spaniards are not able to endure the Horse, and the
Swiss are to fear the foot, when they encounter with them,
as resolute in the fight as they; whereupon it hath been seen,
and upon experience shall be certain, that the Spaniards
are not able to bear up against the French Cavalry, and the
Swiss have been routed by the Spanish Foot. And though
touching this last, there hath not been any entire experience
had, yet was there some proof thereof given in the battle of
Ravenna, when the Spanish Foot affronted the Dutch bat-
talions, which keep the same rank the Swiss do, where the
Spaniards with their nimbleness of body, and the help of
their targets entered in under their Pikes, and there stood
safe to offend them, the Dutch men having no remedy: and
had it not been for the Cavalry that rushed in upon them,
they had quite defeated them. There may then (the defect of
the one and other of these two infantries being discovered)
another kind of them be anew ordained, which may be able
to make resistance against the Horse, and not fear the Foot,
which shall not be a new sort of armies, but change of orders. And these are some of those things which ordained a
new, gain reputation and greatness to a new Prince. Therefore this occasion should not be let pass, to the end that
Italy after so long a time may see some one redeemer of hers
appear. Nor can I express with what dearness of affection he
would be received in all those countries which have suffered
by those foreign scums, with what thirst of revenge, with
what resolution of fidelity, with what piety, with what tears.
Would any gates be shut again him? Any people deny him
obedience? Any envy oppose him? Would not every Italian
fully consent with him? This government of the Barbarians
stinks in every ones nostrils. Let your Illustrious Family then
undertake this worthy employed with that courage and those
hopes wherewith such just actions are to be attempted; to
the end that under your colours, this country may be enabled, and under the protection of your fortune that saying

of Petrarch be verified.

Virtù contr' al fuore Prendera l'arme, e fia il combatter cor-
to: Che l'antico valore Ne gli Italici cor non è morto.

Virtue against fury shall advance the fight, And it i' th' com-
bate soon shall put to flight: For th' old Roman valor is not
dead, Nor in th' Italians breasts extinguished.